The Gift of New Hope
ADVENT

Scriptures for the Church Seasons

ADVENT

The Gift of New Hope

CHRISTOPHER L. WEBBER

An Advent Study Based on the Revised Common Lectionary

Abingdon Press / Nashville

THE GIFT OF NEW HOPE
BY CHRISTOPHER L. WEBBER

An Advent Study Based on the Revised Common Lectionary

Copyright © 2018 by Abingdon Press

ISBN-13: 9781501870859

18 19 20 21 22 23 24 25 26 27—10 9 8 7 6 5 4 3 2 1

MANUFACTURED IN THE UNITED STATES OF AMERICA

Contents

Introduction

Radically different quotations come to mind when I think about the word *hope.*

On the one hand is the Bible, of course. There's a verse in the Epistle to the Hebrews that calls hope "a safe and secure anchor for our whole being"(6:19). In a world in chaos, that is a comforting image. Most of us would like such an anchor. We can also recall the end of Paul's great hymn on love in First Corinthians, in which he tells us that "faith, hope, and love remain . . . and the greatest of these is love" (13:13). Perhaps we remember seeing sets of Bible bookmark ribbons with little symbols at the end of each ribbon for these three "theological virtues": a heart for love, a cross for faith, and an anchor for hope.

Another quotation I remember is from Emily Dickinson, who said that hope is "the thing with feathers." Can you picture an anchor with feathers? But the whole poem is worth reading:

> Hope is the thing with feathers
> That perches in the soul,
> And sings the tune without the words,
> And never stops at all,
>
> And sweetest in the gale is heard;
> And sore must be the storm
> That could abash the little bird
> That kept so many warm.
>
> I've heard it in the chillest land,
> And on the strangest sea;
> Yet, never, in extremity,
> It asked a crumb of me.[1]

At first glance, it might seem that there's all the difference in the world between feathers and anchors, but Dickinson's picture of hope does, in fact, have some of the qualities of an anchor. Hope, as Dickinson writes of it, "never stops," provides warmth in the worst storm, and asks nothing of us. Faith and love, on the other hand, do make demands of us and may not, in our experience, always be there for us in times of storm and crisis.

Let me provide a definition from the online dictionaries of our computer age. Dictionary.com defines hope as "the feeling that what is wanted can be had or that events will turn out for the best."[2] As a verb, its definitions by Merriam-Webster include "to expect with confidence" and "to cherish a desire with anticipation."[3]

That is probably a pretty accurate description of hope as most us think of it, but it differs somewhat from the Epistle to the Hebrews and Emily Dickinson. An "optimistic attitude" may not be an anchor available to us in times of trouble. Hope, from that viewpoint, seems not much different from wishful thinking, and that is hardly an anchor we can rely on in crisis. So how can the "little bird" with feathers provide us with the stability and security we want for our lives?

Before we get too deeply into the question we will focus on for the next five weeks, let's add a few modern perspectives on hope to the discussion. Sometimes popular music is a better expression of current opinion than a nineteenth-century poet like Dickinson or even the Bible. John Lennon probably summed up the popular mood of his era in the song "Imagine," in which he sang of hope for a world without countries, religion, possessions, greed, or hunger. "You may say I'm a dreamer," he wrote, "but I'm not the only one."

There's something wistful and wishful about that song, but it spoke to many people around the world and perhaps even anchored a generation.

The great African American poet Langston Hughes brings us back to Emily Dickinson's "thing with feathers" and may add an essential element to the discussion in his poem "Dreams." In it, he describes a life without dreams as "a broken-winged bird that cannot fly."[4] Here life itself is the bird, and that bird cannot fly without winged dreams, akin to hope, to hold us up.

Think also of the role hope has played in your life. Didn't hope become increasingly central to your life as you moved through school and began to envision a future for yourself? Isn't hope critical in giving birth to children and guiding them through childhood into maturity? And don't smaller goals keep us hopeful as we anticipate vacations and even ordinary events, such as a visit with friends or an evening out for dinner, a sports event, or a concert?

So, yes, hope can hold us up, but is an anchor or a bird the better symbol? Let's leave that unresolved for now and commit ourselves to a five-week exploration that may help us understand better the role hope plays in our lives and, perhaps, find which symbol works best for us. We might even find another symbol that helps us more.

And let's not forget that we are embarking on this journey in Advent, a season traditionally identified with hope, and that we will be finishing our journey with the celebration of Christmas, the day that symbolizes hope for children (and for many adults as well). Let's not forget, also, to ask whether our Christmas hopes have become completely secularized or whether it's still possible to keep Christ at the center of our seasonal hopes.

I hope you have picked up this book and begun to read it with some very real hopes. I hope you will put the necessary work into the adventure to make it productive. The readings we will study provide a rich and nourishing diet for all who want to deepen their life in faith and open the gifts God gives us to guide and sustain us on that journey.

1. From "Hope," by Emily Dickinson, in *Poems, Second Series*, by Emily Dickinson, edited by Mabel Loomis Todd and Thomas Wentworth Higginson (Roberts Brothers, 1891); page 27.

2. *Dictionary.com Unabridged*, Random House Inc., s.v. "hope (*n.*)," http://www.dictionary.com/browse/hope. Accessed April 25, 2018.

3. *Merriam-Webster*, s.v. "hope (*v.*)," https://www.merriam-webster.com/dictionary/hope. Accessed April 25, 2018.

4. From "Dreams," by Langston Hughes, in *The Collected Poems of Langston Hughes*, edited by Arnold Rampersad and David Roessel (Alfred Knopf, 1994); page 32.

Perspectives on Hope

Scriptures for the
First Sunday of Advent
Jeremiah 33:14-16
1 Thessalonians 3:9-13
Luke 21:25-36

"New hope" is the general theme of this Advent study, and we are a people in need of new hope. We find ourselves facing new challenges, and no one can suggest that there are easy answers. In the midst of such enormous struggles as international conflict, terrorism, climate change, immigration, and racial tension—to name a few!—we also have our individual lives to lead, and we need hope there if we are to play any useful part on a larger stage. Some of us may, for various reasons, have strength only for our personal challenges. There are surely times when we can be excused from constant concern with the headlines. Also, if our personal lives lack confidence and hope, we can be of little use to others.

The lessons we have for this first week of the Advent season provide three radically different perspectives on the hope that anchors our faith. The prophet Jeremiah is calling his people to repentance and renewal in the wake of defeat and disaster. In the midst of overwhelming catastrophe, he holds onto a vision of a future filled with hope. However despondent we may be about our national challenges and failures, our role as people of faith is to cling to our knowledge of what God is able to do even through national disaster. The centuries since Jeremiah's time enable us to hold hope with even greater confidence, since we can see how God has worked through other times of crisis to give the church an ever broader vision and renewed strength.

Paul's letter to the Thessalonians is more personal. He writes to friends to speak of the joy that pervades his life and theirs. That joy came to them as they came to know Christ as Savior, and they awaited his return with joy. We surely can share that same joy knowing Christ is already at work in our lives with a strength that cannot be overcome. Paul would encourage us, I believe, to find our joy in the local community, in the immediate challenges that we can face with friends and fellow workers. Joy begins where we are.

The Gospel reading sets our hope in the broadest possible perspective and asks us to think of God's final purpose. It shows us a terrifying vision of ultimate disaster, but even here there is a call to stand up and be confident because, whatever may come, God is at work within world events. As Christians, as the people of God, we can find new hope in knowing what God has done before and knowing also that the best is yet to come.

JEREMIAH 33:14-16

Advent has to do with coming, and coming involves change. However close the relationship, however joyfully we look forward to the visits of parents or children or close friends, when someone else comes into our lives even briefly, our lives are changed by the event. We may need to clean out a spare bedroom, lay in more supplies of food, and cancel other events because our lives will no longer be ours alone to direct. There is joy in looking forward to such reunions, but we also need to prepare for change and take another individual's interests into consideration.

Jeremiah speaks of a life-changing "coming": a "righteous branch," a descendant of David, a ruler who will do what is "just and right." That will definitely change things.

Something we should have learned in recent years is that leaders seldom feel free to do always what is "just and right" even as they understand it. They are subject to the influence of individuals, pressure groups, and "circumstances beyond their control." President Reagan promised to reduce bureaucracy, but the bureaucracy continued to grow. President Obama promised to withdraw from the Middle East, but found himself drawn back in. What would happen if God sent us a ruler who always did what was just and right without fear or favor? Certainly things would change! But is Jeremiah's message a threat or a promise?

THE GIFT OF NEW HOPE

At the time and in his context, Jeremiah's overall message was a threat. He knew that God, unlike human rulers, always does what is just and right. What Jeremiah saw all too clearly was that the Hebrew people were in danger for precisely that reason. God's people had turned away from God in pursuit of their own interests. What Jeremiah understood was that God is just and cannot tolerate injustice. If God's people acted unjustly, God would make no exceptions for them: they would face defeat and exile.

This was not a message Jeremiah wanted to deliver. Jeremiah can be called "the prophet of '*my people.*'" His message of judgment is not of doom for others but for his own people, "my people." He does not point a finger to say, "God condemns you," but rather he says, "*my people* have exchanged their glory for what has no value" (Jeremiah 2:11). "If only my head were a spring of water," Jeremiah writes, "and my eyes a fountain of tears, I would weep day and night for the wounds of *my people*" (9:1, emphases added). When he was first called to speak for God, Jeremiah did his best to avoid the calling and to keep quiet when God commanded him to speak. He had no desire to speak of the judgment facing his own people. But God's word, he said, was like a fire within him that could only burst out:

> I thought, I'll forget him;
>   I'll no longer speak in his name.
> But there's an intense fire in my heart,
>   trapped in my bones.
>   I'm drained trying to contain it;
>   I'm unable to do it. (Jeremiah 20:9)

Rabbi Abraham Heschel said that Jeremiah not only heard God's word but personally felt in his body and emotions the experience of what he prophesied.[1] Jeremiah saw all too clearly the consequences for his people, "my people," if they continued to ignore God's justice, and therefore Jeremiah wept. He saw vividly what was coming. And, of course, he was right. As surely as one plus one equals two, a righteous God plus an unrighteous people equals destruction.

Jeremiah's ministry spanned the last forty-some years of Judah's independent existence, years that led up to destruction and exile in 587 B.C. He saw his prophesy fulfilled. He continued to speak even as the Babylonians were besieging Jerusalem, his beloved city. He went into exile himself, going to Egypt in the aftermath of Jerusalem's destruction. But the text we are given today tells us something else about the God for whom Jeremiah spoke. God judged "my people," Jeremiah knew, because God cares. We set a much higher standard for our own children than for others. If we judge our children and discipline them, it gives us no joy. We weep over their failures even as we judge them. But where there is that sort of judgment, there is also the possibility of mercy and forgiveness. We look for the opportunity to welcome our children back into the family circle. God waits for the opportunity to offer us forgiveness and renewal.

If, then, judgment is coming, so too is a time of renewal and promise. Jeremiah imagines such a time in today's text, Jeremiah 33:14-16. What will that be like?

Here the prophets are at a disadvantage. Perhaps we are too. War and destruction were all too familiar to the prophets; they are still familiar to us. A time of righteous peace and safety is less familiar either to us or to Jeremiah, and Jeremiah can offer us only a hint of what such a time might be like. "Judah will be saved," he tells us, "and Jerusalem will live in safety." Why? Because the Lord will raise up a successor of David and his name will be Righteousness.

Again and again, when they try to see the future, the best the prophets can do is recall the past and the time of David. David was far from perfect. He committed adultery, and he failed to discipline his children. But he knew God's claim on his life, and he knew how to repent. Therefore he was greatly loved and was held up as an ideal for the future. Something like that, "a branch from David's line," is the best Jeremiah can imagine.

So we begin the Advent season, the season of coming, by recalling a time in some ways like our own. We also live in a time of political and moral confusion. We seem unable to find leadership that can embody our deepest values and highest ideals. But Jeremiah, speaking to us out of a similar time, leaves us with the hope that can provide an anchor and the trust in God that enables us to look forward.

We begin, then, with a model from a far distant day that reminds us how, even in times of impending disaster, God has sent prophets to hold up a vision of the future. What is that vision?

Jeremiah is able to offer only a new, improved David. That's not bad, but it's not enough. But Jeremiah gives us a name that we know more about than he. God will send a ruler, Jeremiah says, who will be called, "The LORD Is Our Righteousness." Perhaps Jeremiah saw only a better David; we hear those words and think instinctively of Jesus.

Yet we are also "vision-challenged." What would peace and security look like for us? Would we, like Jeremiah, be satisfied with a new and improved version of some past era, that of Roosevelt or Eisenhower, for example? Would we imagine a messianic age brought about by military superiority, the defeat of all enemies, and the soothing of the passions that inspire terrorism? Advent calls us to be unsatisfied with the mere improvement of the past, mere stability in the present. These four weeks are given us to be renewed in hope, to remember those in the past who have promised us a coming age that belongs truly to God, and to be unsatisfied with anything less. God calls us toward the change that is coming, a change that has a name. We think instinctively of Jesus and ask how the vision comes to life in him.

What deeper identity can we hold on to in the midst of international, national, local, or personal chaos, and how can we let hope in God's promise provide an anchor for us? What vision of hope can you keep your eyes on to give your life meaning and purpose today?

1 THESSALONIANS 3:9-13

We said that "coming" was a central theme of these Advent readings and never more so, perhaps, than in this brief reading from one of Paul's letters. This may well be the oldest document in the New Testament, and it brings us a vivid picture of life in the new Christian community. The coming of Christ is the hope at the center of their life, as it must be of ours. We will need to say more about hope, but for now we can concentrate on the nature of the coming that we hope for.

What did it feel like to be a Christian in a world where there had never before been Christians? Can you imagine? To become a Christian now in America is usually to enter into an established community with an accepted pattern of life. For the first Christians, it must have been more like a constant process of invention. Some, of course, were Jews; they had been members of a synagogue and knew that pattern of life. The new Christian community inevitably would adopt some aspects of that pattern; but all of it would be open to question and subject to change. In my own experience, whether in a congregation or in the larger community, I have often thought, "If I could reinvent this community from scratch, I would do it differently." But once a pattern is set, significant change is difficult. The Thessalonians were starting from "Square One." What must that have been like?

Hanging over whatever pattern they adopted was that word "coming." Even as they developed a pattern of community life, they could never settle into a comfortable rhythm because more change was on the way. Paul, first of all, prayed that he would be able to come back soon. So Paul would be coming back and no doubt would have guidance for them. Whatever they decided to do needed to be provisional against Paul's coming and the possibility of new instructions. But more important still was the promise of Christ's coming "with all his people" (verse 13). The Greek word here translated as "people" is literally "holy ones." So we are talking about an event beyond the normal flow of history. We may picture that in various ways, but it is enough to realize that it will be a "coming" that transforms all the normal patterns of life. If Christ comes with his holy ones, what changes in our comfortable life together will be needed? Two thousand years have gone by, but our patterns remain provisional, remain under judgment. If I have wanted to reinvent the communities familiar to me, how might Christ want to reinvent our community? It is, after all, his community, not ours. Have we thought about that? It's easy to measure our Christian communities against the standard of other Christian communities, but the familiar question, "What would Jesus do?," is surely relevant. If Jesus should come—and he is as near to us as he was to the Thessalonians—what would need to be changed? What would survive?

The answer to that question surely begins with two other key words in this passage: love and joy. Love is the cause and joy is the result. Paul prays that God will cause the Thessalonians—and us—to increase in love for each other and for everyone (verse 12). I wonder how often we look at our congregation in such simple and basic terms. We tend to look at our outreach programs and special events and worship, preaching, music, and education programs and ask how we could do these things better. But suppose we just asked ourselves, "Do we love each other enough?" Assuming the answer is "No," unless you belong to a congregation that has achieved perfection, one where the kingdom has already arrived, what might we do to grow in this most basic of all aspects of Christian life? How do we go about growing in love?

The answer would seem to be as simple as it is obvious: Paul roots that growth in prayer. Every one of us has room for growth in prayer (verse 10). And that prayer, centered in love, must produce deeper, fuller, and more caring human relationships. Most relationships in a congregation are not, if we are honest, deeply loving. We work together, we enjoy one another, we support one another (though there may be room for improvement even there), but do we deeply love one another? Do we care for each other with the same passion with which God, we are told, loves us? There are people I see every Sunday. I nod to them, maybe exchange pleasantries about the weather; perhaps we serve together on a committee or work together in some outreach program. I like them, but do I love them? Do I love them as God, I trust, loves me?

But Paul doesn't stop there in his prayer. He prays as well that God will "cause you to increase and enrich your love for each other and for everyone"—for *everyone* (verse 12). Not just for the "in" group, not just for our fellow church members, not even just for our fellow citizens—though that's enough of a challenge in our current political climate—but for everyone. Of course our congregations have outreach programs. We may feed the hungry and house the homeless. We may well support outreach to other countries and continents. We may care about the people we serve. But do we love them? Can God "increase and enrich" our love "for each other and for everyone?" Beyond those with whom we have such relationships, do we love also those with whom we have no relationship or whose lives are set against us in active hostility?

I am a pessimist. I doubt we can do it. But Paul is an optimist and has no doubt that the little band of Christians in Thessalonica can do it. He expects results from them and surely he would expect results from us. Suppose we take this one step at a time and begin with whoever it is, whatever group it is with whom we are at odds, whose way of thinking we cannot understand. They may be within our congregation, or perhaps in our community, or out there somewhere in our national life. How can we love them? How can we moderate our reaction to them? How can we look for something in common, some way to reach out, some way to build bridges? It must be obvious that a society so bitterly divided over so many things is not sufficiently undergirded by Christian, Christ-like love. And the provision of love's impact surely begins with you and me.

So Paul is coming back to the Thessalonian church, and he prays that he will find them growing in love. More importantly, Christ is coming, and Paul prays that he will find us sufficiently developed in holiness that we may be "blameless" in that day (verse 13). Paul suggests no new programs, just prayer, but prayer that will change things, change us, change you and me so deeply and fully that we will be prepared for that coming we hope for. That hope and that prayer will bring to fulfillment God's purpose for us and for all the world.

Are you an instinctive optimist or an instinctive pessimist? Can you identify yourself with those early Christians whose lives were filled with joy simply because they knew God had chosen them for a purpose? What can you do to deepen your life of prayer?

LUKE 21:25-36

The Bible is many things, but it is not an "answer book." It does not provide us with dates and times for the end of the world. Many good people have studied the Bible and made detailed calculations about when the end would come. They gathered followers, even sold their possessions and waited—and were proven wrong. The Bible is not that kind of book.

Look carefully at the Gospel reading for this first week of Advent. A first glance, a quick reading, might give the impression that Jesus is providing his disciples with specific information about the end of the world. He is not. It is unfortunate we have not been asked to read this passage in a larger context, because earlier in this same chapter we would have found the disciples asking Jesus for information about the coming messianic age and being warned to be careful, not to be deceived, and not to follow those who tell them "it's time" (Luke 21:7-8). Then Jesus talks about cataclysmic events, events that we might identify with the hurricanes and tidal waves that have become almost commonplace in our times (21:25-26). But Jesus never makes a one for one connection. When these things happen, he says, stand up and lift up your head because your redemption is near (21:28). But "near" leaves a lot unspecified.

In the larger chapter, there are specific events mentioned that took place long ago, as well as others that are unlikely ever to happen. "Jerusalem surrounded by armies" (verse 20) has often happened. "Not even one stone . . . left upon another" (verse 6) seems unlikely ever to take place; some of the stones of the first-century temple mount still rest one on another and are visibly in place at the Western Wall, or "Wailing Wall," in Jerusalem. The people of Jesus' time were eager to see signs of the end, but Jesus spoke of them only vaguely and warned people constantly not to follow those who thought they had specific information. To pin our hopes to that sort of sign is to ask for information that the Bible does not provide.

We should also notice that whatever biblical passages there are describing earth-shaking events as signs of the end, there is a radically different tradition that seems more persistent and widespread in the life of the early church. This alternative tradition speaks of an end that will come upon us suddenly and unexpectedly "like a thief in the night." Before the words were spoken that we found in this week's reading, in the same Gospel of Luke Jesus told his disciples that "if the homeowner had known what time the thief was coming, he wouldn't have allowed his home to be broken into. You also must be ready, because the Human One is coming at a time when you don't expect him" (12:39-40). Even in this week's passage, we are warned not to let that day come on us "unexpectedly, like a trap" (21:34-35).

That tradition, of an end time that comes as suddenly and unexpectedly as a "thief in the night," appears in other New Testament writings as different as 1 Thessalonians 5:2-4, 2 Peter 3:10, and Revelation 3:3. The spectacular passages about signs in the sun, moon, and stars, on the other hand, appear only in a few select Gospel passages. Some scholars point out that such predictions of catastrophe were common in Jesus' time and doubt that these words originated with Jesus himself.

What then are we to learn from this passage and its description of events that will cause people to "faint from fear and foreboding of what is coming upon the world" (Luke 21:26)? We can benefit from a reminder that our stable earth is a bubble in an infinite universe, that it will at last fall into the sun, that whatever cataclysmic events take place now or in some future time, God is the Creator and holds the whole creation in hands of love. Most especially, we can benefit here at the beginning of Advent from a thoughtful discussion of such passages as this in light of our constant need to be "shaken up." We need to be reminded how fragile this earth is and how certainly we are unable to erect lasting monuments to our accomplishments and ourselves. If we place our hope in earthly things, we will be greatly disappointed. If we place our hope in human predictions of "end times," even more certainly—Jesus warned us—we will be left looking foolish as many well-intentioned Christians have been both in time past and in our own day.

Our theme is hope. Hope is an anchor, a source of stability in unstable times and amid both natural and human events that remind us how little security is to be found in earthly things. If we are dismayed by "nations in their confusion over the roaring of the sea and surging waves," there is plenty about which to be dismayed. There is every reason for people to "faint from fear and foreboding of what is coming upon the world." But we, as followers of Jesus, are not called to find our hope in an armament race in response to such events, or in withdrawal into bomb shelters. Those provide no lasting anchor of hope.

Notice, then, that there is in this week's passage one rock of confidence, one anchor of hope, one sure ground on which to build even though "heaven and earth . . . pass away" (verse 33). Jesus' words, we are promised, will "not pass away." What words are those? Not words about dates and times that can give us a false confidence, but words about meaning and purpose. If there are frightening events around us, we have instructions as to how to respond: "stand up straight and raise your heads, because your redemption is near" (verse 28). Christians, now as then, are those who know where security is to be found and can provide an anchor for their society by remaining calm in the midst of chaos. In the midst of chaos, we have a promise, an anchor, an unfailing hope that far exceeds what this world can offer.

Georgia Harkness was a Methodist theologian and the first woman to teach theology in an American seminary. In the early days of the

Cold War, she wrote a hymn that is one of the finest statements of hope ever composed. One verse of that hymn will provide an appropriate focus for us as we go on to think in more depth about the hope God has given us in Christ:

> Hope of the world, who by thy cross didst save us
> from death and dark despair, from sin and guilt,
> we render back the love thy mercy gave us;
> take thou our lives, and use them as thou wilt.[2]

Empires – how many?

Questions for Discussion

1. When you think about your hopes, are they centered in your private life or in God's purpose? What difference does it make?

2. What does "hope" mean to you? Does it suggest to you something more like a wish or does it suggest something stronger, a true "anchor" for our lives? When asked to explain hope, what specific examples arise in your mind?

3. What signs of hope do you see in your community, where people or institutions are working on real answers to the issues facing us?

4. What are your hopes for this Advent/Christmas season? How are these hopes grounded in God's past and future purposes?

5. In what ways does your congregation provide an anchor for your life and the lives of others?

6. Think about your local community and discuss places where you see hope at work. Or perhaps you see only areas where you hope to see hope at work, where despair is prevalent and hope is needed. Is your church involved in bringing hope to such places? If not, how could it be?

Suggestions for Group Study

A Poetic View of Hope

Turn to the Introduction of this book and find the poem "Hope is the thing with feathers," by Emily Dickinson. Form groups of two or three, and assign each group one verse of the poem. In each group, take the assigned verse and rewrite it as a simple, clear English sentence. After everyone has finished, come back together and read each group's sentences aloud. Then, discuss the following questions:

1. Did you understand the poem better by rewriting it in your own words?

2. What insights does this poem have about hope? How does it reflect the hope we celebrate at Advent?

3. Which of today's biblical readings most closely portrays hope like the bird that Dickinson envisions? Why? How would you describe the hope we see in the other two biblical passages?

Make a Hope Chest

Construct a "Hope Chest" for daily use by making a box or other container, into which you will place Bible verses and signs of hope from the world around you. Each individual may make his or her own, or the group may construct one working together. The container could be as simple as a shoebox, gift bag, or even an envelope, or it could be something more substantial. Be creative!

On separate slips of paper, list at least seven Bible verses, some at least from this week's readings, to which you might turn for hope. If possible, also list seven signs of hope in the world around you, also on separate slips of paper. Put the Bible verses and signs of hope into the Hope Chest, and each day this week draw out two slips of paper for reflection and inspiration.

As you read each slip of paper, think about how this verse or sign reflects our Advent hope in Christ.

Prepare for a Visit

Imagine that you have just received a letter from Paul saying that he will be coming soon for a visit. As a group, decide what plans you will need to make for the event, and create committees to carry out your preparations (services, community relations, ecumenical relations, hospitality, and so forth). Use Paul's words in 1 Thessalonians 3:9-13 to guide you. After 10 to 15 minutes of planning, discuss the following questions:

1. How would Paul respond to the preparations you have made for his visit?

2. How are your preparations for Paul's visit different from other potential visitors, such as colleagues, friends, or family? What about a visit from a celebrity, or the President of the United States?

3. Now, imagine that instead of Paul coming for a visit, it is Jesus Christ returning to the earth in glory. How would your plans change?

4. How can we make these preparations right now, on a daily basis, so that we are not caught unawares when Christ returns "like a thief in the night"?

Closing Prayer

Anchor our hope, O God, not in the abilities you have given us or the security we may have found in the material things of this world, but in the biblical witness to your faithfulness in times past and to your purpose for us in times to come. Help us to align our hopes with your purpose and to offer ourselves in your service. May your grace come and this world pass away! Amen.

1. From *The Prophets*, by Abraham Heschel (Harper and Row, 1962); pages 116–117.
2. From "Hope of the World," words by Georgia Harkness, *The United Methodist Hymnal* (The United Methodist Publishing House, 1989); 178.

Finding New Hope in History

Scriptures for the
Second Sunday of Advent
Malachi 3:1-4
Philippians 1:3-11
Luke 3:1-6

Once again, we find ourselves with three radically different passages: There is the epic sweep of biblical prophecy in the first reading, the intimate message from Paul in the second reading, and the very specific ministry of John the Baptist in the Gospel. As in the first chapter, we have the opportunity to look at hope from several angles. By coming to understand better the role hope has played in other eras and other lives, we see more clearly how hope plays a role in our lives today.

As the new lectionary has become more widely used, it has become customary in many denominations to hear three lessons on Sunday morning, but some complain that it is "too much," more than they can take in. Some clergy agree and only use two readings or even one. Some preachers make it their practice to include references to all three readings in their Sunday sermon, while others prefer to focus on one reading or even a part of one reading. We can discuss that another time, but having three readings surely does provide a variety of perspectives and may make it likelier that we will find a word in this abundance of words that speaks specifically to us. It may be worthwhile to say something here about the way the pattern of three readings can enrich our understanding.

Often, as with this set of readings, it is the Old Testament that provides a historical focus and, if nothing else, reminds us that ours is a historical religion. Our knowledge of God comes not primarily from a set of enshrined teachings, but from our understanding of God at work in history. We respond to what God has done, not only to what

God says. It is easy to lose sight of that focus on history and action if we omit the Old Testament. We find words of comfort and reassurance in the prophets who speak to us today, of course, but it adds depth to their words to notice how they are spoken at a specific time to people facing specific challenges.

The Epistle may be the easiest reading to take out of context, since Paul is writing with advice that is often not linked to particular historical circumstances. This week, however, Paul mentions the fact that he is in prison. He is not simply writing useful advice from a comfortable chair, but living with the consequences of his teaching. What he taught upset people sufficiently to have him locked away more than once.

So, too, with the Gospel: We can hear Jesus' words and teachings and forget the historical context behind them. But Jesus spoke to specific people in a particular place and time. This week's Gospel reading, though its focus is on John the Baptist, reminds us of the historical dimension at the outset by giving us a specific time and place.

History matters. It is because God has acted in history that we can expect confidently that God will act in our time and our lives. Ask what difference these readings make to yourself and your church at the time and place we inhabit. God acts in history, and that grounds our hope in the present and future. How is God acting now? What new hope can we find in these readings for ourselves today?

MALACHI 3:1-4

There are two great divides in the history recorded in the Old Testament. The first is the period of slavery in Egypt, which divided the time of the patriarchs from the time of settlement in Israel and the eventual creation of a united kingdom under David. The second is the exile in Babylon, a period that reshaped God's people and made them more aware of their nature and calling. It might be said that before that time they had been a tribe that happened to have a special knowledge of God, while afterwards they knew themselves to be first of all a chosen people who happened to have a tribal or national identity. In the previous chapter, we heard the words of Jeremiah on the eve of the exile. In this chapter, we hear the words of the prophet Malachi as he brings God's word to bear on the completely new situation after the exile: a time of rebuilding, but also of disappointed hope.

Different dates are commonly given for the years during which the people of Judah were in exile in Babylon, but we know that the first deportation from Jerusalem took place in 597 B.C., and people began to return from exile in 539 B.C. For most of the exiles it was more than half a century from the time they were carried away to Babylon until the time when they able to return. In those fifty to seventy years, many of the exiles had thought again and again of their homeland, and they had imagined a triumphant return and a time of renewed and greater glory. Many also had died and their children had never seen the homeland their parents spoke of; they had only the dream not governed or limited by any real experience of the place. Their hopes and expectations, as a result, had grown beyond what could easily be fulfilled so that, when they returned, an initial time of joy was followed by the inevitable letdown and discouragement. The prophet Malachi dealt with a people who had come home again and rebuilt the city walls and Temple, only to discover that the human beings who inhabited the renewed city were still all too human. One commentator sums it up this way:

> They built the temple and waited and waited but there was no glory. Instead there was . . . poverty, oppression, unfaithfulness . . . pride, indifference, . . . skepticism. . . . Malachi tried to rekindle the fires of faith in the hearts of his discouraged people.[1]

Perhaps it would be better to say that in a time of discouragement, God sent Malachi to restore the vision and to assure the people that God was still at work in their lives. God was still at work in their lives, but that was not necessarily a reassuring and comforting thought. If we hope for God to be at work in our lives, Malachi told them, we must accept the consequences: a radical judgment on our lives by a God who comes to purge and renew.

Such times of discouragement, or times when vision is lost, are inevitable unless we are willing to live without a vision. Think how, after the First World War in which Americans were sustained by a vision of a "war to end all wars," we settled instead for the economic prosperity of the Roaring Twenties only to see it collapse in the Great Depression. Or think how, after fighting for the vision of "four freedoms" in a world at peace in the Second World War, we found ourselves trapped instead in a Cold War. It has been said that "where there is no vision the people perish," but where there is a vision it can turn easily into discouragement when we are unprepared to deal with the reality of human self-centeredness and blindness.

Malachi is speaking to people like us who would like to have the vision without the commitment. Again and again, Malachi points to the difference between the life God expects of the people and the halfhearted way they have responded. They bring an offering, but not of the best (Malachi 1:8). They bring a tithe, but not a full tenth (3:7-10). But how, Malachi asks, can they expect God to fulfill the vision when they have not committed themselves to that vision? How can they expect God to serve them when they fail to honor God? Malachi understands that this failure can only lead to disaster, to a "great and terrifying day of the LORD" (4:5).

It is against that background that we need to read today's lesson and understand why the prophet calls for a day of reckoning in Malachi 3:1-4. The God they long for will certainly come, Malachi tells them, but that coming day will be a day of judgment, of purging, without which there can be no renewal of the covenant.

Isn't this our problem as well? We still like to think of ourselves as a Christian people, but something is missing as it was in Malachi's day. We find ourselves bitterly divided where Christians might be expected to be most united. God is the Lord of life; life is a gift, and all life belongs to God. Yet Christians line up on both sides of issues where life is at stake: abortion, the death penalty, health care, and gun control. No doubt there are deeply committed Christians on both sides of these issues. But might we not hope for a discussion in which there is, at the very least, real listening on both sides and a willingness to hear and to understand the other person or people so that we can work together toward a peaceful resolution of such issues? Failing that, what can we expect except exactly what Malachi prophesied for his people: a sudden judgment, a coming very different from the coming we hope for. At some point, God will certainly come, and come in judgment. Can we really hope for such a coming, or should we fear it? Malachi is speaking to a people who long for God to come. He tells them they may be surprised by the reality of it. God will not act simply to give people what they want. God will act to bring about God's purpose, and that purpose may be very far from the popular expectation. In verse 2, Malachi asks:

Who can endure the day of his coming?
Who can withstand his appearance?

Is this, then, a coming to hope for? Clearly Malachi believed that his people were in no condition to look for a coming that would bring them joy in their present situation. They must instead expect a painful purging that will enable them to bring God acceptable offerings. And what then of us? Are we in a better position than Malachi's people to look forward with hope, or do we also need to be purged and purified? Might we hope God will not come but will leave us alone until we can reform our lives?

Do you have an active hope for a greater presence of God in your life? To what extent are you willing to hold up your life to God's judgment? Could you "endure the day of his coming"?

PHILIPPIANS 1:3-11

Here, as with last week's second reading, we are put in touch with one of the earliest Christian communities. The city of Philippi had been established as a Roman colony, and many of its most important citizens would have been retired army officers, citizens by virtue of their army service though not necessarily Roman by birth. A substantial portion of the people of the city, however, would not have been Roman citizens at all, and many of them would have been slaves with no hope of the privileges that went with Roman citizenship. It is against that background that Paul tells the Philippians "our citizenship is in heaven" (Philippians 3:20). Roman citizenship may be a nice thing if you have it, like Paul; but, then and now, the primary allegiance of Christ's followers is to the community of saints in heaven and on earth. Though Paul was proud of his Roman citizenship, it did not provide his primary identity. Roman citizenship divided him from many of the Philippians, but membership in heaven in Christ united them and made any other citizenship a minor trifle.

Notice, then, the immediate nature of our Christian hope. Heaven is not a hope for some distant future but a present reality. We are united now with "all the company of heaven" in the heavenly citizenship that provides a strength and unity no earthly citizenship can give us.[2] Roman citizen or not, Paul finds himself in a Roman jail and separated from the community he loves. As a citizen of heaven, however, Paul remains free and united with the beloved community in Philippi.

We know it was in Philippi that Paul first preached the gospel in Europe, but there is great uncertainty as to where Paul himself was located when he wrote the letter to the Christians there. He speaks of "my time in prison" (verse 7) and many therefore assume he was in Rome at the end of his ministry, since we know he was in prison at that point. But there were also prisons elsewhere in the empire, and the references in the letter to frequent communications and travel between Paul and the Philippians lead some to suggest that Paul may have written from Ephesus. If Paul was writing from Ephesus, the Letter to the Philippians may have been written as early as A.D. 54 or 55; but if he wrote from Rome, it was probably some five to seven years later and toward the end of his life.

Whatever the circumstances may have been, it is clear that Paul feels a close kinship with the community in Philippi. He speaks to them with a special fondness and draws parallels between their suffering, his suffering, and the suffering of Christ. Nowhere else does Paul speak so much about himself and his suffering, but he does so here not to boast or complain, but for the sake of his congregation in Philippi. He wants them to understand that suffering can be productive. He wants them to see what was accomplished through Christ's suffering and death, as well as through Paul's own suffering, so that they also can endure and bear a faithful witness. "God," he tells them (and also, perhaps, us) a little later in the letter, "has generously granted you the privilege, not only of believing in Christ but also of suffering for Christ's sake" (1:29). Suffering is not a punishment or a failure or a setback

THE GIFT OF NEW HOPE

in this situation but an opportunity, even a gift, to use in the work God has given us.

"You are all my partners in God's grace," Paul writes (1:7), and it is not what we call today a "limited partnership" in which we share some of the advantages but with a limited risk. No, Paul takes this beloved community into a full partnership "both during my time in prison and in the defense and support of the gospel." One commentator, Markus Bockmuehl, draws a sharp contrast between the gospel Paul proclaimed and the "health and wealth gospel" promoted by some evangelists today. "Paul's understanding of grace," Bockmuehl writes, "does not depend on life, liberty and the successful pursuit of happiness."[3] Notice also that although Paul clearly is very fond of the people of Philippi, he does not speak of loving them himself but of sharing with them the love of Christ. "I feel affection for all of you," he writes, "with the compassion of Christ Jesus" (1:8). Does our love for each other have that dimension? Lots of people fall in love and lots of people are very good friends, but to love others as Christ loves them is surely something far deeper and stronger, and it is that love that Paul feels toward the people of Philippi.

We should notice also Paul's prayer. It was a standard part of his opening words in his letters. Just as we might say, "I hope you are well," so Paul says, "I pray for you." Our good wishes, however, are very short term; Paul thinks in terms of a final accounting: "I pray . . . (that) you will be sincere and blameless on the day of Christ" (1:10). It's a nice thing to be well at the moment and even better to be faithful at the moment, but what matters is who we are at the end. Here again we need to think in terms of a new Christian hope that is transforming life now. Dorothy L. Sayers, someone once told me, noted that "the best kept inns are on the through roads." There are unfortunately all too many people who have no sense of direction and purpose, and therefore settle for whatever they find. It's the people who are going somewhere who make a difference here and now. Paul wants the Philippians—and us—to keep in mind the hope of our calling. This world needs people whose eyes are set on a better world and who therefore can transform this one now.

A growing concern in recent years is the number of Americans who see no hope of improving their situation in life. Christianity has been caricatured as telling people to settle for "pie in the sky" and a reward hereafter. Paul was writing to people whose role in life was much more fixed than ours has been. What do you think he would write to us about that? Would he tell us not to worry because our "citizenship is in heaven," or would he challenge us to bring that citizenship to bear on our earthly community in a way that makes a difference?

Do you think of your faith in terms of specific issues and goals, or primarily in very general terms such as "a positive attitude"? What is the difference?

LUKE 3:1-6

One of the biggest surprises that can come from actually sitting down to read the biblical story of Jesus is the discovery that the Christmas story is an afterthought. Two of the four Gospels, Mark and John, never mention Jesus' birth. Matthew concentrates on the coming of the wise men and mentions the actual birth of Jesus only in passing. Even Luke, many experts believe, seems to have added his story of the Nativity later. It is, of course, Luke's story of the birth of Jesus that brings us the shepherds and angels, but there is a clear stopping point at the end of Luke Chapter 2. When Luke began to write the main narrative of Jesus' life and ministry in Chapter 3, he instinctively began in the same place as Mark and John: with the ministry of John the Baptist. For all four evangelists, this is the real beginning of the story. Notice how carefully this passage begins (3:1-2): We are given the date and place in a very deliberate and formal way. Luke is a historian; he is telling us about specific, historical events, and he starts by letting us know that he has done his research. Make what you will of the infancy narrative, which Luke dates much less exactly (see Luke 2:1-2); what starts in chapter 3 is real history. And remember also that this dating has to do not only with the beginning of John's ministry but also with Pilate and Herod. These rulers held power at the beginning of Jesus' ministry and also at the time of his death. Once again, we should stress the fact that Christian hope is not wishful thinking. These things really happened in a datable, historical world, and therefore we can look forward with a confident hope that the God who has acted for our good in the past will also act for our good in the future.

In this real world something strange happened: God's word came to a man called John, and he began to preach repentance (3:2-3). Notice how this Gospel puts it: "God's word came." The initiative is with God, not John. John did not decide to preach; he responded to a word that came. God took the initiative. More specifically, that word came to John "in the wilderness." What was he doing there? He seems to have been waiting. Why else would someone be in the wilderness except to break away from the usual pattern of life and be open to a word that might come? So John was there waiting and open to God's initiative. And the word came, and John responded.

We sometimes imagine John out in the wilderness waiting for people to come, but that's not Luke's understanding of the situation. It was God's word that came to John, and when it came John didn't wait for people to come to him. He went throughout the region of the Jordan River calling people to his baptism (verse 3). God doesn't send a word to you as a private possession. When the word comes, you go; and so John went. He went "calling for people to be baptized."

Now, John didn't invent baptism. There were people down by the Dead Sea called Essenes who practiced baptism. There seem to have been a number of Essene communities, and the way of life they practiced differed from one to another. Their baptism seems to have been sometimes for initiation into the community and sometimes simply for ceremonial washing or purifying. From what we are told in today's passage, John's baptism may not have been radically different from other baptisms, like those the Essenes practiced, being administered not far away. We are told that he preached a baptism for people to "show that they were changing their hearts and lives and wanted God to forgive their sins" (verse 3). We will hear more about John's message next week. So far, we hear simply of a baptism that will demonstrate repentance, a change of heart, a desire for forgiveness.

Christians have had different ideas of baptism at various times and places. There are some for whom baptism is like the one John announces here: a baptism to show God that we want forgiveness and intend to lead a new life. Much of the emphasis falls on our action and commitment. Other Christians think of baptism primarily as an act of God by which forgiveness and new life are given even to infants. We must remember that John's baptism is not necessarily the same thing as Christian baptism, so we need to look elsewhere to settle that issue. The point here is that people are being called to take stock of their lives, realize how far they have fallen away from God's will for them, and make the changes that are necessary to embrace God's will here and now. John is calling people to change their hearts and lives, and they are responding.

We must notice also, however, that Luke sets this ministry in a very large context. This is not just an obviously needed call to repent. That would undoubtedly be appropriate at most times and in most places. But Luke tells us that what John was doing occurred "just as it was written in the scroll of the words of Isaiah the prophet" (verse 4). He is, in other words, taking us back over five hundred years to hear words spoken by one of the greatest of Israel's prophets, suggesting that John's ministry is part of the long-expected drama Isaiah spoke of in which "all humanity will see God's salvation" (verse 6). This is, in other words, no local event, no more or less routine call for spiritual renewal. This is part of God's age-old purpose for the human race and John, as Luke tells the story, is a key actor in that drama, one who has been sent to be that "voice crying out in the wilderness" that would "prepare the way for the Lord."

And one more point. By linking this event to Isaiah's words, Luke sets it not only in the age-old drama of God's relationship with the human race, but also in terms of God's purpose for the whole of creation. Nature itself bears witness to what God is doing. As the prophet said, "Every valley will be filled, and every mountain and hill will be leveled" (verse 5). We live in an age when the filling of valleys and leveling of hills is commonplace, but in our ruthless domination of the natural world we have begun to threaten our own existence. Luke imagines a world in which nature itself bears witness to God's action in history; we inhabit a world in which we are beginning to see that we cannot simply impose our will on the natural world without consequences. A true messianic age would be one in which human beings learn to practice stewardship of creation, to act reverently toward the natural world, to see God's presence in a human history that moves us toward what Pierre Teilhard de Chardin, a Jesuit theologian and scientist, called "the Omega Point." In that final stage, the whole universe will attain a higher level of consciousness, expressing ever more completely the purpose of the

God who created it.[4] John the Baptist is a key figure in the long history of witnesses who call us to repent and renew our relationship with the Creator God who works in history toward that purpose.

In what ways are your Christian hopes too limited? How can you place your story on a canvas as large as Luke envisions?

GROUP STUDY GUIDE

Questions for Discussion

1. How would you describe the Christian vision for the present and the future? What gives our life together in Christ purpose and direction? What must change for us to realize this vision?

2. As you look at your church, your community, or our world, do you see more reasons for disappointment or for hope? What about as you look at your own heart and life?

3. If the "day of the Lord" were to happen tomorrow, would you welcome it or fear it? What aspects of our society would have the most to fear? Who would have the least to fear?

4. What do you think Malachi would have to say to us about what we should expect from the Lord's coming?

5. Have you ever suffered or experienced hardship as a result of your faith in Christ? What was that experience like? What might Paul say to you to offer encouragement?

6. Paul tells the Philippian church that "our citizenship is in heaven." Name some areas where your citizenships in church and state come into conflict. What does it mean for you to prioritize your heavenly citizenship?

7. When and where were you baptized? Was it your own decision? If not, can you point to a moment when you realized and welcomed the significance of your baptism? If you do not know, do some family research to find out if, when, and where you were baptized.

8. What significance does baptism have in your life or your family? What about in your church? In society at large? How does baptism reflect, or lead to, a changed heart and life?

9. Our faith is centered on the way God works in history. How do you see God at work in world and national events? How is God at work in the life of your church?

10. In what ways do you hope God will work in our world today?

Suggestions for Group Study

God and a Fresh Start

Go around the group and have each member describe a time when they have made a "fresh start," undertaking a major change in life. Examples might include starting college, starting a job, getting married, having a child, moving to a new city, changing careers, ending a marriage or relationship, and so forth. After each person has provided an example, discuss the following questions:

1. What was your vision for this new stage of life as you began it? What hopes and fears did you have, and what provided direction or purpose for you?

2. How did your faith shape these expectations? In what way did you see this new venture as a calling from God?

3. How did your experience confirm or alter your vision? What mistakes did you make, or what disappointments did you encounter? How did your expectations change?

Have group participants keep these experiences in mind as one member rereads Malachi 3:1-4 aloud slowly. After you've finished reading the passage, discuss these questions:

1. What might God have done in your life to "purify" your fresh start experience, "clearing the path" and recommitting you to your vision and calling?

2. Would this process have been painful or welcome? Why?

3. What difference would this purification have made at that point in your life?

4. What difference would such a word from God make in your life today?

Respond to John the Baptist

Take a moment as a group and brainstorm all the different roles and vocations that each of you fulfill (career, mother/father, brother/ sister, child, friend, volunteer, mentor, and so forth). If possible, list these for display on a markerboard or large sheet of paper. Now imagine your congregation has gone out to hear John the Baptist preaching in the wilderness. Briefly go through each role and discuss how you would respond to John in this role (note that not all roles will apply to every person). What sins would you confess? What changes would need to take place in your heart? How would you change your life as a result of John's message and your baptism?

After the discussion, have each participant name one thing they'll do this week to "show that they [are] changing their hearts and lives." Commit to making these changes, and check in with one another each week of this study to keep one another accountable.

Closing Prayer

Time and again, O God, you have given your people a vision of your purpose, offering us hope that you will enable us to serve you and work with you toward the fulfillment of that vision. Renew in us the commitment made at our baptism, that we may be a baptized and hope-filled people united in serving you. Let your kingdom come in us, and let us center our hope in your purpose. Amen.

1. From *Micah-Malachi*, by Ralph L. Smith, Word Biblical Commentary (Thomas Nelson, 1984); pages 299–300.
2. From *A Service of Word and Table I*, in *The United Methodist Hymnal* (The United Methodist Publishing House, 1989); page 9.
3. From *The Epistle to the Philippians*, by Markus Bockmuehl (A & C Black, 1997); page 63.
4. See *The Phenomenon of Man*, by Pierre Teilhard de Chardin, translated by Bernard Wall (Harper & Row, 1959).

Joy Breaks Through

***Scriptures for the
Third Sunday of Advent***
Zephaniah 3:14-20
Philippians 4:4-7
Luke 3:7-18

The story is told of a Jewish holy man of the seventeenth century who went to a certain city and asked the people how the rabbi conducted the prayers for Yom Kippur, the great day of penitence and prayer. They said to him, "He chants all the confessions for Yom Kippur with joyful melodies." So the mystic sent for the rabbi and asked him, "Why do you sing the confessions joyfully?" The Rabbi responded, "Lo, a servant who is cleaning the courtyard of the king, if he loves the king, is very happy cleaning the refuse from the courtyard, and sings joyful melodies, for he is giving pleasure to the king." Said the holy man, "May my lot be with yours!"[1]

Here we are more than halfway through the short Advent season. We have less than two weeks before Christmas, and we should be penitent because we are so far from ready for the coming of Jesus into our lives. We are far from ready, but joy inevitably comes breaking in. Joy is the dominant theme in two of the three readings this week, the joy of preparing for the King and "giving pleasure" to our Savior.

In ancient tradition, this third Sunday of Advent is called Gaudete Sunday, and *gaudete* is the Latin word for rejoice. Some churches use rose colored vestments to brighten the day instead of the usual purple, and the third candle on the Advent wreath may also be rose colored, symbolizing joy. This change of mood is like the way joy bubbles up when you plan a surprise for someone and can barely keep the cat in the bag until the big moment. Joy breaks out. It can't be contained. It's hard to understand how Christians at some times and places have been seen as joyless people, and how penitence and sorrow have often overwhelmed Christian faith.

Advent is a season of mixed penitence and joy. To prepare for a celebration takes planning, work, and discipline, but joy keeps breaking in. We are preparing, after all, for a birth, not a death. We are preparing to celebrate a gift of life. When purple is used in Advent, it is sometimes called a penitential color, since it's used for that reason in Lent. But we do well also to remember that kings wear purple; it is a royal color and some say we bring it out to decorate the King's palace as for a coronation, a celebration. (Some churches in fact prefer to use blue in Advent to avoid the heaviness of purple, and to symbolize heaven breaking in with the birth of Christ. It is also Mary's traditional color, and Advent is often treated as Mary's season.)

This is, then, a time when the readings tell us to "lighten up." Why is it that Christians sometimes find that hard to do? The twentieth century English theologian Charles Williams once said, "Christianity, like all religions, is, frequently, almost unmitigated boredom or even a slow misery, in which the command to rejoice always is the most difficult of all."[2] These readings command us to rejoice. Is it really that hard for us to rejoice, so hard in fact that we need to be commanded to do it? If so, why? We need to ask such questions as we read, hear, and think about the readings for this week.

The Gospel, at first glance, strikes a very different note with its report of the ministry of John the Baptist, but the three readings simply provide different perspectives on the same issue: preparing for Christ to come. The first two readings emphasize the attitude of joy while the Gospel emphasizes the very practical work we need to do to be ready. All the better for us if we can do this work joyfully, like the rabbi who sang the Yom Kippur confessions.

ZEPHANIAH 3:14-20

Suppose more than two thousand years from now historians looking back were to attempt to analyze the changes in American society from the presidency of Franklin Roosevelt to that of Ronald Reagan. Suppose they were to attempt to understand a transition that took place: from the Roosevelt era's enormous reliance on government to solve problems to the Reagan era feeling that government itself is the problem. And then suppose these future historians were to try to understand how some of our prominent authors fit into that span of time, asking how the writings of John Grisham, Stephen King, and John Steinbeck reflect their period of history. Something like that is the task confronting scholars who set out to tell us about the prophet Zephaniah.

To look at the prophecy of Zephaniah involves us in a period of some thirty years of history in ancient Judah, from about 640 B.C. to 609 B.C., a slightly shorter time span than Roosevelt to Reagan and a period involving only one king as compared to nine presidents. Josiah, the king who ruled Judah in those years, came to the throne as an eight-year-old child, and it's reasonable to assume the real government was in the hands of his regents until he was old enough to take full command (2 Kings 22:1). After he had reigned for eighteen years, sudden and dramatic changes began to take place. New voices began to be heard and the idols that had been installed in the temple were swept away. In the process of repairing and renovating the temple, a scroll was discovered that laid out a law for God's people. This book seems to have been either the Book of Deuteronomy or something very much like it, in which were found the laws said to have been given to the people by Moses. Josiah set out to follow this law and to purify the temple and eradicate the places where idols were worshiped (2 Kings 22:3–23:25; 2 Chronicles 34:3–35:19).

The small Book of Zephaniah comes from this time and contains in its three chapters prophecies of judgment as well as a glorious promise. Some scholars find it hard to believe that such different visions could come from the same mind. Certainly, the first few verses of Zephaniah could scarcely be more negative, as God promises to undo the fifth and sixth days of creation (Zephaniah 1:2-3):

> I will wipe out everything from the earth, says the LORD.
>   I will destroy humanity and the beasts;
>   I will destroy the birds in the sky and the fish in the sea.
>   I will make the wicked into a heap of ruins;
>   I will eliminate humanity from the earth, says the LORD.

On the other hand, after that there's nowhere to go but up! King Josiah, with a vision of pure worship, set about first to destroy and then to rebuild. His predecessors had allowed pagan practices to be adopted and used even in the Temple in Jerusalem. To adopt the strict standards of Deuteronomy involved radical change, and Josiah set out to bring that change about. The story is told in the Second Book of Kings, Chapter 23. A typical verse goes like this:

> He removed the Asherah image from the Lord's temple, taking
> it to the Kidron Valley outside Jerusalem. There he burned it,
> ground it to dust, and threw the dust on the public graveyard.
>
> (2 Kings 23:6)

Burning, breaking, and smashing, Josiah set out to make the drastic changes needed, and Zephaniah seems to have given strong support to Josiah's reforms. In broad terms, Zephaniah reflects the time of enormous change through which he lived. Scholars debate whether he prophesied before Josiah began his reforms or afterwards. That seems less important than seeing the big picture and recognizing that Zephaniah was closely connected to the work of reform that Josiah initiated.

How is it possible, some scholars ask, to imagine one prophet denouncing the present in such drastic terms and also prophesying such a glorious future? But enormous changes were taking place and Zephaniah was fully involved in his world, encouraging the destruction needed to clear the way for a new day and holding up the promise of the glorious time to come. And what a glorious time! The contrast between destruction and renewal could not be more sharply defined, nor the joy of the promised time made more vivid:

> Rejoice, Daughter Zion! Shout, Israel!
> > Rejoice and exult with all your heart, Daughter Jerusalem.
> >
> > (3:14)

> The LORD your God is in your midst—a warrior bringing
> victory.
> > He will create calm with his love;
> > he will rejoice over you with singing (3:17).

THE GIFT OF NEW HOPE

And that joy will be for everyone:

> I will deliver the lame;
> I will gather the outcast. (3:19)

Imagine one of those all-too-frequent stories we follow on television of a child lost, possibly kidnapped, and then returned. We have seen that kind of joy. Or think of the joy we see when a soldier returns to his or her community after serving in military action. But it is not only our joy that is the focus here; it is God who is joyful and singing because of us! Do we really appreciate how much God cares? Jesus said, "Joy breaks out in the presence of God's angels over one sinner who changes both heart and life" (Luke 15:10). That's joy over *one*, but what if there were two or three or a million? What if you and I were to help lead a parade of returning children of God coming back where we belong?

This Advent season is an opportunity for us to reenact in our own lives and our own communities the drama Zephaniah has set in front of us, the contrast between the tearing down of idols and the restoration of a true, pure, and heartfelt worship of Almighty God. Josiah's idols were simple to deal with from a physical point of view: Drag them out, smash them to powder, scatter the powder, and they are gone. But not all idols are material. What idols draw us from true worship? What business or recreation or self-indulgence captures us when God is not, in the words of the familiar hymn:

> thou and thou only, first in my heart,
> great God of heaven, my treasure thou art.[3]

Our Advent theme is "new hope." That was what Zephaniah placed before his contemporaries, and it is what he sets also before us. Few have portrayed that hope so eloquently, and it is small wonder that we turn to it on this third Sunday of Advent when the joy ahead of us begins to break through. We might wonder whether the prophet needed to spend so much time in warnings and threats of disaster. Isn't the hope of joy motive enough? How can we not respond to a God who loves us so much? What can we possibly cling to that would keep us from giving God such joy? Another familiar hymn seems to sum it up:

The dearest idol I have known,
Whate'er that idol be
Help me to tear it from Thy throne,
And worship only Thee.[4]

What aspects of your life receive more of your time and energy than they deserve, drawing you away from loving and serving God? How can you properly order these things, ripping them out if necessary, so that they don't become idols?

PHILIPPIANS 4:4-7

We return this week to Paul's letter to the Philippians, remembering how suffering—the gift of suffering—is of key importance in this letter. That theme, introduced at the beginning of the letter, continues to be a central aspect of what Paul has to say. Against that background, toward the very end of Paul's letter, this week's reading stands, Karl Barth once said, as "a defiant 'Nevertheless!' that Paul sets like a full stop against the Philippians' anxiety."[5] In other words, Paul has written up to this point about the use and meaning of suffering, but he cannot end without setting that in the larger context of resurrection faith. Yes, Jesus suffered for us. Yes, Paul and the Philippians have suffered. Yes, we also may need to endure suffering. Nevertheless! Nevertheless, the last word is that we can and must "be glad" or "rejoice" because we are followers of a risen Christ who passed through suffering into eternal life. Hope is, once again, the critical element. It is because of that hope that we are able to be glad.

This attitude of hope and joy has consequences for our relationships with others, for our relationship with God, and for ourselves. Karl Barth has a striking way of describing the difference gladness makes for our relationships with others. The reading says, "Let your gentleness show in your treatment of all people" (Philippians 4:5). We live in a world where gentleness is not often encountered, but Barth says that Christians are people "who have been made . . . mellow, 'beaten to a pulp,' as opposed to the non-recipients of grace, who can still be stiff and bristly."[6] If the world seems sometimes to wear us down, might that be God's way of making us mellow? How often do we encounter gentleness in our daily lives? How often do we act with gentleness toward others? How different would our world be if more of us were mellow and fewer of us were bristly?

As for our relationship with God, we are told that "the Lord is near" (verse 5). Is Paul talking about the Second Coming? He doesn't say so. There is a sense in which any thought about the Second Coming is a distraction. Surely more important on a day-to-day basis is the reality of the Lord's nearness now. Our hope is not fixed on a distant horizon but on a God nearby. God is near us now and therefore Paul says we need not be anxious, but should come to God with requests, petitions, and thanksgiving (verse 6). Barth says we must be beaten to a pulp, and John Calvin says, "We are not made of iron, so as to be unshaken by temptations."[7] If we are trying to face the world in our own strength, we are not likely to be very successful. Indeed, we are likely to be shaken more than a few times by world events and by our own relationships with others. Therefore John Calvin says we need to turn to a God nearby in prayer. We can do so in confident hope.[8]

Notice particularly that our prayer is to include not only petitions but also, from the very beginning, the giving of thanks. In most of our relationships there is a sequence: First someone does something for us, then we thank them. It's not like that with God. From the first moment, there is thanksgiving. God has always been acting in our lives for our good. Wherever we go, whatever we do, God is there first. We might even say that it is because God has already given us cause for thankfulness that we dare to bring petitions. Because God has been at work in our lives, we dare to come asking for more.

Then comes peace. For ourselves, the gladness Paul commands us to have brings a peace beyond any the world can give. When we know the nearness of God and respond in hope with prayer and thanksgiving, peace follows. Peace is a result of our self-offering; it comes at the end. *The United Methodist Book of Worship*, like the similar books of every church that uses set forms of prayer, provides these words of Paul as a concluding prayer or blessing: "The peace of God that exceeds all understanding will keep your hearts and minds safe in Christ Jesus" (verse 7).[9] John Calvin wisely reminds us that "the peace of God does not depend on the present aspect of things." No, it depends on a Christian hope that enables us go on our way rejoicing even in the midst of chaos and to be glad in the knowledge that God is near.

We are in the position, perhaps, of men and women in a lifeboat, survivors of a shipwreck, who hear a message on their only cell phone just before the batteries fail: "We know where you are and are on the way." The storm may still rage, we may not even be in touch with our rescuers, but we can relax and be at peace, even be glad, because we know we are not alone, not abandoned. We are confident in the hope we are given and are able to be gentle toward others and joyful in the midst of chaos, because we know our redeemer lives and is near at hand.

How does God give you a peace "that exceeds all understanding"?

LUKE 3:7-18

A woman who took part in the demonstrations in Ferguson, Missouri, in 2014 wrote afterwards of how she had gone with great hope. But she found her hopes turned to fear as she moved out onto the street and found herself facing policemen armed with tear gas, flash grenades, and rubber bullets. "Hope," she wrote, "is always frightening. It opens us to disappointment."[10]

Advent is the most dangerous time of the year. When else do tension levels rise so high? When else are we so vulnerable to disappointment? It's a statistical fact that the death rate rises in December. The old and the lonely, especially, find it hard to live through the memories on the one hand and the loneliness on the other. "No man is an island," said John Donne; "I am involved in mankind." Or perhaps he should have said, "I need to be involved in mankind."

It's hard to be alone. And it's hard for all of us, even in the best of circumstances, to be secure in the knowledge that we are not alone, that someone else truly cares.

Part of the tension of the season, surely, is the effort we feel compelled to make to earn the love we can't quite believe we deserve. The madness of the Christmas shopping season must be partly a result of that need to reach out and to be drawn in to be part of a community in which we are valued and cared for—yes, and possibly even loved. For without love, we die.

And that, I think, is why the crowds went out to listen to John the Baptist. The Gospel for this third week in Advent is one of the strangest we will ever hear. It's fire and brimstone with a sardonic chuckle at the end. Here's John's opening line:

"You children of snakes! Who warned you to escape from the angry judgment that is coming soon?" (Luke 3:7)

Isn't that a great way to begin a sermon? It ought to get your attention! But let me give you my own version of the first few lines of John the Baptist's sermon:

"You brood of vipers! The Messiah is on the way
and he has an axe all sharpened to cut you down
and unquenchable fire to burn you up."

And then, as I said, there's that sardonic chuckle at the end:

With many other words John appealed to them, proclaiming good news to the people. (Luke 3:18)

I would put it this way: "He had lots of other good news too."

Well, if that's the good news, we probably don't want to hear the bad news! But in fact this *is* good news if you always thought nobody cared. John's fundamental message was: "God cares about you. God is not satisfied with you, but God cares."

There is always a crowd for the preacher of condemnation because everyone hopes he's talking about someone else. Politicians often find their best approach is to "go negative," to talk about how terrible the other candidate is. I'm sure the crowds that went out to hear John were glad to hear him condemning someone else. And he did. He condemned the soldiers, the tax collectors, the priests, business people, lawyers, farmers, housewives. He was very specific. And finally no one was left out. When the crowds asked him, "What then should we do?" He answered, "Whoever has two shirts must share with the one who has none, and whoever has food must do the same" (Luke 3:10-11).

John the Baptist had a specific message for everyone: "Whoever you are, there is something you need to do. And there's unquenchable fire for those who fail to do it." People asked and he told them: "You specifically need to do *this*. This what God asks of *you*." And that is good news. Do you sometimes doubt that God cares, that anyone cares? You couldn't doubt that if you listened to John. He let you know: Yes, God cares. God knows exactly what your life is like and where it is missing the mark and what you need to do. God knows. God cares.

And what does that mean, I wonder, for you and for me? If John's first command to the crowd was, "Share," wouldn't that be his first word to us as well? Certainly there are far too many today at home and abroad who are hungry and homeless, and far too many at home and abroad who could share much more than they do. If we have a Christmas budget, is sharing with others a part of it: I mean others outside our family and immediate circle?

If John could see the Black Friday crowds trampling each other in their desperation to get what they have to have if their Christmas is to be successful, wouldn't he wonder whether we are trying to buy love for ourselves rather than give love to others?

And wouldn't John be as specific with us as he was with the soldiers and tax collectors who asked what his word was for them? Are you an employer? Deal justly. Are you an employee? Be content. Are you a lawyer? Use your skills for the powerless. Are you a banker? Take no unfair advantage. Are you in health care? Then truly care.

Now these are not rules for the kingdom. This is just basic housekeeping. This is just preparation. The Messiah is coming and when the Messiah arrives, we will be called to a whole new level of living. When the Messiah arrives, we will be called up to the full potential of human living, to pure, self-giving love.

But John is not the Messiah. John is just here to make sure we are not totally embarrassed when the Messiah does come. John is here to give us a warning, a chance to get ready. But this is just a warm-up for the real thing. And those who don't get warmed up won't be ready for the heat. For "he is like the refiner's fire," said the prophet Malachi, and "Who can endure the day of his coming? Who can withstand his appearance?" (Malachi 3:2). Who can expect to survive and stand in the presence of God? That is the challenge of John.

Now, John the Baptist is a prophet in the great tradition of the Old Testament prophets, messengers who announced justice and pointed to the reign of God as the ultimate standard by which we are judged. The prophets come to speak for God. They are people who see clearly what most of us see only dimly: that this is God's world; that we are God's people; and that God does care deeply about our use of God's gifts and our response to God's love. God cares about each of us. John the Baptist proclaims that care by preaching justice. John wants us to know that what we do matters, that how we live matters, that our lives have value. God values us, and judgment is evidence of that value. No one bothers to judge or value someone or something they don't care about. God judges because God cares. And that *is* good news.

That's why there is that sardonic chuckle at the end. "John proclaimed fire and brimstone and lots of other good news."

We need to hear about judgment, but we need to remember also the rest of the good news. We know—and it is what Advent is preparing us for—that God's care goes far beyond judgment, far beyond any words at all. God's loving care comes down at last to God's own loving presence in our midst, his birth in a stable, his death on a cross, the power and promise of resurrection life. God's love reaches out to the loneliness we all feel and says, "Relax, don't worry; no madness of Christmas shopping can earn the love we need, nothing we ever do can deserve it, but it's ours all the same simply because God loves us." We are not alone. The message of the season is Emmanuel: God with us. Hope is dangerous. It open us to disappointment. But God does not disappoint us. God cares. God cares. God cares.

What are your priorities at the moment, and how do they reflect the need to be ready to receive Jesus in our hearts at Christmas? Are you able to hear the word of judgment as well as the word of promise?

GROUP STUDY GUIDE

Questions for Discussion

1. What idols would a modern King Josiah want to pull out of our churches or national temples (which might be stadiums or office towers)? What message of joy and hope might Zephaniah bring along with that destruction?

2. Josiah ground sacred images to dust, and Jesus spoke of the coming destruction of the Temple. Churches often find that they have to spend so much maintaining infrastructures—physical and institutional—that they have nothing left for outreach. How do you recognize when the status quo has become an obstacle to your mission?

3. What cleaning or destruction needs to happen in your own life? What do you hold up as an idol, and how is God calling you to a transformation in your inner life?

4. Can you think of times in your own experience when hope has been frightening because it opened you to disappointment? What is the reason for hoping in such instances nevertheless?

5. Why does gentleness seem to increase with age or experience? How have you become more gentle or mellow over the last few years, and how has that affected your relationship with Christ?

6. In what ways do we pursue gladness or happiness in our lives? Why is gladness so often elusive or short-lived?

7. How can the joy of the Advent/Christmas season be a lasting joy? What is your source of enduring gladness?

8. Why do we need to be commanded to rejoice? What takes the gladness out of faith, and how can we prevent this from happening?

9. Consider the following quotation, from above: "The prophets come to speak for God. They are people who see clearly what most of us see only dimly." Are there such prophets today? How would we recognize them? What message might they bring to us?

Suggestions for Group Study

Keep the Focus on Christ and Our Joy

Some people try to control the madness of the shopping season by limiting themselves to catalog or online shopping, or by setting an early deadline to complete it so that they can give their attention to the real purpose of the season. Go around the group and ask how each member handles it (or doesn't). Come up with new ideas as well. What can participants learn from one another about how to keep Advent and Christmas centered on Christ? What have you learned or experienced during this study that will help you do so?

As a group, decide on the top two or three ways to maintain a sense of joy in Christ this Advent season, including any new ones you may have devised. Through the next two weeks leading up to Christmas, adopt this practice. Check in with one another to offer encouragement and prayers, and to share one another's joy.

Advertise for John the Baptist

Choose two group members to engage in roleplay, with one person designated as Member A and the other as Member B. Member A should invite Member B to come and hear a great new preacher, John the Baptist. Member B should be skeptical, asking for information about his message, what makes him a good preacher, and so forth. Spend one or two minutes with A trying to persuade B. Next, select two more group members to reenact the roleplay, again with A trying to convince B to hear John the Baptist. After two or three rounds, stop and discuss the following questions:

1. Which "advertiser" for John the Baptist was the most convincing? Why was the advertiser convincing?

2. What other arguments could have been used to come hear the preacher?

3. Have you ever used any of these arguments to invite someone to come to church with you, or to consider your Christian faith? Why or why not? If so, how well did it work?

4. Based on your discussion and the reflection on Luke 3:7-18 above, what made John the Baptist effective?

5. How can we translate John the Baptist's message to our world? What would be the purpose in doing so?

Closing Prayer

Let the hope you have given us, Eternal God, fill our hearts with joy as we remember your mighty acts in ages past, and as we look forward with new hope to the day when you will fill all human hearts with the knowledge of your redeeming power. As you guided Josiah to cast out the idols of his day, guide us to recognize the false gods that take your place in our lives. As you enabled your servant Paul to rejoice even in his sufferings, so enable us also to rejoice in whatever times of testing we face. As you sent your word to John in the wilderness, send now your word to us and help us to hear it and respond to it with new hope and ever greater joy. Amen.

1. From *Let Us Rejoice! It's Yom Kippur*, Yom Kippur Morning Sermon, 2014 / 5775, by Kim Harris, *http://images.shulcloud.com/515/uploads/staff/SermonsArticles/harris-2014-10-yom-kippur-morning---let-us-rejoice-its-yom-kippur.pdf*. Accessed May 5, 2015.

2. From *Religion and Love in Dante: The Theology of Romantic Love*, by Charles Williams (Dacre Press, 1941); page 91.

3. From "Be Thou My Vision," *The United Methodist Hymnal* (The United Methodist Publishing House, 1989); 451.

4. From "O for a Closer Walk with God," *The Methodist Hymnal* (The Methodist Publishing House, 1964); 268.

5. From *The Epistle to the Philippians*, by Karl Barth, translated by James W. Leitch (Westminster John Knox Press, 2002); page 120.

6. From *The Epistle to the Philippians*, by Karl Barth, translated by James W. Leitch (Westminster John Knox Press, 2002); page 121.

7. From *Commentaries on the Epistles of Paul the apostle to the Philippians, Colossians, and Thessalonians, translated and edited from the original Latin, and collated with the French version*, by John Calvin, translated by John Pringle (Edinburgh: The Calvin Translation Society, 1851); page 119.

8. From *Commentaries on the Epistles of Paul the apostle to the Philippians, Colossians, and Thessalonians, translated and edited from the original Latin, and collated with the French version*, by John Calvin, translated by John Pringle (Edinburgh: The Calvin Translation Society, 1851); page 120.

9. See *The United Methodist Book of Worship* (The United Methodist Publishing House, 1992); pages 50 and 151.

10. From "Marching into Danger," by Shannon Craigo-Snell, in *The Christian Century*, September 17, 2014, *www.christiancentury.org/article/2014-09/marching-danger*. Accessed June 9, 2015.

Hope in Unexpected Places

Scriptures for the
Fourth Sunday of Advent
Micah 5:2-5a
Hebrews 10:5-10
Luke 1:39-55

Sometimes it almost seems as if the church doesn't get the message: "Hey, it's Christmas! Haven't you noticed?" Every store in town has its seasonal decorations up and the sound system endlessly repeating holiday songs, but most of the churches are slow to join in. Last week the Scripture readings stressed the theme of joy, which fit well with the outside world. Now, however, with only a few days left, the readings seem to turn away from the rising tide of excitement outside and ask us to think quietly and seriously about the reason for it all. By this time, many churches seem to give up the effort to move at a different pace and let the last pre-Christmas Sunday become a time to "pre-celebrate." They don't get much help from these readings that give us a rather restrained bit of prophecy, a very sophisticated bit of theological thinking, and the quiet story of the meeting of two pregnant women who will have much to celebrate shortly, but not yet. "Not yet" might be the theme for this last week of Advent. But just as it's hard to explain to a small child that "it isn't your birthday yet," so it is almost impossible to explain to those who have been conditioned by weeks of accelerating emphasis on Christmas that we're not there yet; we have some serious thinking and praying to do first.

Is it worth it? Shouldn't we just give in and get on board the secular express? Well, what if the churches got together and said, "Enough already! Let's go with the flow and celebrate Christmas early like everyone else"? It might be amusing to see what the merchants thought when they found a few days of selling eliminated! And what real damage would it do? After all, December 25 is not the actual date of Jesus' birth. As the early Christians took over the pagan festivals of the winter solstice, why couldn't we take over the pagan celebrations of our day? What if we celebrated Christmas on Black Friday and preempted the selling season altogether? There's really no reason not to—except that we would lose out on the time we never have enough of anyway to do the inward and prayerful preparation that makes the real difference. And, of course, it would only take the stores a year or so to adjust to the new dates and leave us just where we were before, except a month earlier.

It's not easy to be a Christian at Christmastime and find ourselves out of step with a world that thinks it's celebrating our festival. But it is a valuable gift to be reminded that Christianity is about transforming the world, not conforming ourselves to it. And as today's Scripture readings show, the truly important things are those that the world considers insignificant. Let's accept the gift thankfully and take a close look at the pattern of our lives, asking ourselves, "Am I doing this because I am a follower of Christ or because it's what everyone else does and I never stopped to ask 'Why?'" If we can make time to do that, it might just be the most valuable gift we can give ourselves at this very special time.

MICAH 5:2-5a

There is an old story of a poor rabbi in Cracow, one of the oldest cities in Poland, who dreamed one night that there was a great treasure buried under the bridge in front of the royal palace in Prague. So the rabbi set out for Prague to see whether he could acquire this treasure for himself. When he arrived in Prague, however, he found that the bridge was very carefully guarded, and he saw no way to get at the treasure without being noticed and stopped. So for several days he loitered by the bridge and finally managed to fall into conversation with the captain of the guards. As they talked, the rabbi found himself admitting that he had dreamt there was a treasure there. The captain laughed and thought the rabbi was a fool. "I once had a dream," he declared, "that told me to go to Cracow and search for treasure under the stove of a certain Jewish man." When the captain said the name of the Jew he dreamt of, the rabbi recognized it as his own.[1]

Isn't that the story of Advent and Christmas and, indeed, of the way we often live our lives?

Human life is often frustrating, and our hopes exceed our achievement. We look for some missing element to transform our lives: a king, a savior, a political leader or party, or maybe a lottery ticket. We look for the perfect gift to give or receive that will make this Christmas different from all other Christmases. We look for something whose possession will complete our happiness and fulfill our lives. We may call it security, peace, contentment, power, fulfillment, accomplishment, achievement, joy, or satisfaction. We have many names for it, but do we really know what and where it is? All too often we center our hopes in some distant and unreachable place: under the bridge at the royal palace and not in our own home.

There is a very human tendency to be impressed with grandeur. When Jesus led his disciples up to Jerusalem, they were overwhelmed by the size and magnificence of buildings, far beyond what they had ever seen in Galilee. One of them exclaimed, "Teacher, look! What awesome stones and buildings!" But Jesus responded, "Do you see these enormous buildings? Not even one stone will be left upon another. All will be demolished" (Mark 13:1-2).

I recently read a book by A. M. Allchin, an English theologian, who was commenting on the survival of the Welsh language and traditions in spite of all attempts to eradicate them. He compares it to American treatment of Native Americans and writes of our unwillingness or inability to hear the "other," to see things from a different point of view. Especially, he wrote, we are insensitive to things that are small and judge them in terms of size and power. He doesn't claim that this is a uniquely English or American tendency, but suggests that we have had such power for so much of our history that this trait may be magnified in us.[2]

As an American of significantly English background, that judgment makes me uncomfortable. All the more reason to pay attention and beware—be aware—of the possibility that we, like the disciples, may be too easily blown away by power and pomp and prestige, too ready to think that might makes right, that power goes with goodness, that wealth equals virtue.

Today's Old Testament reading gives us a radically different perspective: God's perspective. The prophet Micah is speaking:

As for you, Bethlehem of Ephrathah,
    though you are the least significant of Judah's forces,
        one who is to be a ruler in Israel on my behalf will come
        out from you. (Micah 5:2)

This perspective is hardly unique. We need to read the Old Testament with an eye to similar passages. There are many such passages in which God chooses the weak rather than the strong, the small rather than the large, the unknown instead of the famous.

Perhaps we can learn from modern medicine. Medical people these days have the ability to look into the human body in new ways and see things we could not have seen before. They can inject a dye or a radioactive isotope, and suddenly a bone abnormality can be seen that had been invisible. I sometimes think that the early Christians began to read the Hebrew Scriptures in a similar way, as if they had injected a dye that lit up passages never noticed before. It's as if, after the Resurrection, they went on a scriptural Easter egg hunt and found scattered all through the Scriptures verses never noticed before, which jumped out at them when they looked with eyes opened by the life of Jesus. Again and again, they found verses that told them that God had worked and would work through the small and insignificant and overlooked, even the rejected and despised.

One of the Psalms says:

You rebuke the arrogant. . . . (Psalm 119:21)

The prophet Zechariah was told that God's purposes would come about,

"neither by power, nor by strength,
but by my spirit. . . ." (Zechariah 4:6)

Christians would also have noticed God's word to the people in Deuteronomy:

It was not because you were greater than all other people that the LORD loved you and chose you. In fact, you were the smallest of peoples! No, it is because the LORD loved you. . . .
(Deuteronomy 7:7-8)

Once it had been possible to overlook such statements—but not after knowing Jesus. In weakness God came into the world and died for us. In weakness, without armies or material weapons, the Church overcame the Roman Empire.

The German philosopher Friedrich Nietzsche thundered against what he saw as the weakness and suffering promoted by Christianity, calling for a "transvaluation of values" (or "revaluation of values") to give high regard again for the strong and masterful.[3] But Christianity has continued to insist, like Saint Paul, that our strength is in weakness:

> Therefore, I'm all right with weaknesses, insults, disasters, harassments, and stressful situations for the sake of Christ, because when I'm weak, then I'm strong. (2 Corinthians 12:10)

This is not to say that we aren't still tempted to use the world's weapons, to build the biggest churches and draw the most influential people. If we do draw the homeless and hungry, it's often to a side door during the week, not the main door on Sunday.

Yet still it seems that the weak in this world often control the strong. The United States has a gross domestic product over eight hundred times that of Afghanistan, but what use is that strength when it comes to shaping events in the Middle East?

Magicians know how easy it is to draw our attention away from what is really happening, often with show or flair to hide their true actions. If it's only a magician's trick, it doesn't matter. But what does matter is our tendency to let irrelevancies shape our lives, to focus our attention and energies on the show and drama of a world that is passing away instead of the quiet revolution that God is always bringing about from within. Micah bids us instead to pay close attention to Bethlehem of Ephrathah, the "least significant," to recognize and welcome a King whose birth lies far from the grandeur of Jerusalem or Rome.

How do you suppose Herod felt when his wise men told him to send the magi to Bethlehem (Matthew 2:4-8)? "Go to an insignificant little place like Bethlehem? Nothing worth anything comes out of there!" The lives of those in Bethlehem scarcely mattered to Herod, which is why the magi found Jesus but Herod never did. He spent his days in the palace and had the feeling that he was shaking the earth. But he died and was forgotten—except for the fact that he was on the wrong side when it mattered.

We have such choices ourselves. We have lots of things to do these days that seem terribly important: places to go, gifts to wrap, parties to attend. Vitally important: If we don't get them done, our world will come to an end. Or so the story goes.

But when we come to church on Christmas Day, God will be there with all the strength and love we will never find elsewhere.

Are you looking for salvation in Bethlehem of Ephrathah? How is God seeking you in the seemingly insignificant things?

HEBREWS 10:5-10

The Sunday before Christmas is a challenging day for the preacher. It's officially the fourth Sunday in Advent, but many churches, having no strong tradition of weekday services, call this day "Christmas Sunday." After all, the department stores have been celebrating Christmas for weeks; maybe it's not too late for the church to join the celebration! Even churches that call it the fourth Sunday of Advent may have a Christmas pageant at this time, or the beautiful Service of Lessons and Carols.

Such churches are not likely to pay much attention to this passage from Hebrews. Even congregations in churches that use this reading are not likely to hear a sermon about it. The references to "burned offerings" and "sacrifices" don't resonate immediately with thoughts of Christmas and the birth of a baby. This selection is a small segment of a long and complicated discussion in Hebrews, and those who assigned it to this Sunday are complimenting us in expecting us to understand its importance. We are, however, given an opportunity here to step aside for a moment from the rush of celebration around us and focus on the meaning and purpose of the event. The birth of a baby is beautiful, and angels are lovely, and sheep and shepherds are romantic . . . but what is it all about? The passage from Hebrews sums it up in one brief repeated phrase: "I've come to do your will" (verses 7 and 9). After the shepherds and wise men go on their way, we are left with a baby who will grow to be the man who will change all life forever. Jesus has "come to do your will, God" (verse 7). He has come to serve God perfectly, and to enable him to do that, God has "prepared a body" for him (verse 5).

It's the preparation of that body that's critical. Christianity at the core is about just one thing: God among us in a human body. We call it the *Incarnation*, and without it you have just one more religious system with some inspiring teaching and excellent ideals but nothing that makes a real difference in the relationship between God and the human race. Other religions are centered on a book or a body of teaching. Christianity is centered on Jesus, God in human flesh, God in a human body. It's all very well to know the Bible, but it's more important to know Jesus. Only the Incarnation makes a radical difference in our human situation by bridging the gap between the divine and the human and enabling us to see and touch a body in which God is fully present among us. Christianity is a three-dimensional faith.

Former Archbishop Temple of Canterbury once said, "Christianity is the most materialistic of all great religions."[4] That may or may not explain the rise of capitalism in the Christian West, but it would seem to explain why Christian missionaries were almost as likely to build schools and hospitals as churches. Other religions could see the suffering of bodies "ill housed, ill clad, ill nourished" (Franklin D. Roosevelt, "Second Inaugural Address") and console themselves with the thought that it was "only" the body that suffered and the soul would be set free at last from its bondage to the body. But Christians spoke of a resurrection of the body and needed to minister to the body even now.

It was, after all, bodies that God had created out of the soil of the Garden of Eden, and those bodies were shaped in the image of God. A rabbinic tradition tells us that when any human being walks on the street "a procession of angels passes before each person, and the heralds go before them, saying, 'Make way for the image of God!'" (Deuteronomy Rabbah, 4:4).

This also, of course, explains why the celebration of Christmas is so materialistic. What other religious festival of any faith is so universally merchandised? There's a reason for it. God has expressed love for us in the most material way possible, and we inevitably respond by showering material gifts on one another. But the essential gift remains the human body; only by caring for the human body can we respond appropriately. It makes no sense to shower dolls and ties and teddy bears and jewelry on one another while human bodies continue to suffer. Charitable organizations understand this and come asking our help at this time especially—as they should. The generosity of our response is an accurate way to measure our understanding of the Incarnation.

To do God's will a body was necessary. It still is. As God's love was embodied in Jesus of Nazareth, it must also be embodied in us, and it must reach out through us to the needy bodies visible on our television screens and in our immediate neighborhoods. Before we get any closer to Christmas, we need to remember what the celebration is all about and examine our priorities. Are we prepared to celebrate the day with a good conscience, knowing that we ourselves are truly incarnating the love of God, making God visible in our bodies by our ministry to the bodies of others?

Two very different voices, those of Dwight D. Eisenhower and Dr. Marin Luther King Jr., have summed up this message:

"Every gun that is made, every warship launched, every rocket fired signifies, in the final sense, a theft from those who hunger and are not fed, those who are cold and are not clothed."[5]

"Any religion . . . not concerned with the slums that damn them, the economic conditions that strangle them, and the social conditions that cripple them is a dry-as-dust religion."[6]

Through the ages, human beings have felt a need to atone for their failures and come into a greater unity with God. Sacrifice and offering are widespread phenomena for that reason. Christians also often attempt to make things right by gifts and offerings. But what God seeks is not our gifts but ourselves, in particular our bodies to be united with the body of the Child born in Bethlehem. It is the church's role to incarnate Christ in every community. If, when the Christmas celebration is over, Christ has not been born anew in our community and in each one of us, we have failed to hear the Christmas gospel. Now, with only days left, we need to hear the message of this reading.

Here's a hymn I have written that may help us focus on the issue:

1. From Nazareth to Bethlehem
        came Mary and her spouse
    And settled in a cattle shed,
        unwelcome in a house;
    And Christ in homeless people now
        lacks shelter from the rain
    While those who live secure and warm
        can spare no room again.

2. From Bethlehem to Egypt then
        Christ's family took flight
    While many other children died
        as Herod showed his might;
    And children suffer still today
        while governments stand by;
    Lord, give your people hearts to act
        and ears to hear their cry.

3. From Egypt up to Nazareth
        the holy family went
    And found a home and work to do,
        no longer indigent;
    But laws and borders separate
        the work and workers now;
    Can we find ways to change the laws
        and what they will allow?

4. Lord, open human minds and hearts
        and give us eyes to see
    How we might work together now
        to change society,
    To let your children grow in peace
        with no one homeless still
    And opportunity for all
        in keeping with your will.

Think about the community you live in. How do human bodies and organizations incarnate God's love, or how do they fail to do so?

LUKE 1:39-55

I grew up in a very small town in upstate New York, and I remember that the local paper had a weekly column of social notes. The column contained reports like: "Mary Jones dropped in on Susan Smith last Wednesday for tea" and "Billy Johnson had six of his friends over on Saturday to celebrate his seventh birthday." I doubt that those columns will still be read two thousand years from now. Yet the Gospel reading this week asks us to take note of just such an event: Mary, the wife of Joseph Carpenter, went to visit Elizabeth, the wife of Zechariah Priest. Two unimportant women spent some time talking about the babies they were expecting. It happens all the time. Why does it matter?

We might begin by asking how we decide what matters. One reason we go to church is surely to check our value system; one reason we read and listen to the Bible is surely because it gives us a value system that seems to make sense. It tells us what God considers important and what therefore we also should consider important.

Some people might tell you that what's important to them is their bank account or their golf game. If so, I think their values are badly skewed.

We know what the Bible tells us about money, for example: that the love of it is the root of all kinds of evil (1 Timothy 6:10). To consider money important is to have a value system out of sync with God's.

Jesus, we know, cared a great deal about the right use of money, but he cared nothing for money simply as a possession. Jesus cared about people, but even there he had a radically different value system than most people around him. He was often criticized for his choice of personal relationships. He sat down to eat with public officials and sinners. He reached out to lepers and made no distinction between Judeans and Samaritans, Jews and Gentiles. And it is all highlighted in the Gospel today, where we hear of a couple of obscure women in a distant corner of the world who are expecting babies.

If you were God and planned to change the world, whom would you choose? In a world ruled by men, you would certainly choose a man. In a world ruled by Rome, you would probably choose a Roman. But God choose a Jewish woman. It would be hard to imagine someone less important by the standards of Mary's world and really, if we are honest, even by our own standards. But Mary became the most important woman in world history because she was God's choice. God chose her. God said, "You are important to me." And God's valuation has proved to be true. She was and is important because God called her, chose her, empowered her.

And listen again to Mary's response:

> He has looked with favor on the low status of his servant.
>   Look! From now on, everyone will consider me highly favored
>   because the mighty one has done great things for me.
> Holy is his name. (Luke 1:48-49)

That comes first: I will be who I will be not because of power or skills or influence of any kind, but because of what God has done. And it has implications. If God has made one like Mary important, then the world is transformed and changed. If God has chosen Mary, the world's values are undone: the mighty are put down and the unimportant are lifted up; the hungry are fed and the rich are sent away with their investments suddenly worthless (verses 52-53). Whether you think Mary actually said these words or that Luke imagined her saying them, it is still astounding how they understand already that the world has been changed forever: "Everyone will consider me highly favored. . . ." There is a new order of things, a new value system in the world.

It did not begin with Mary. This is the outline of a pattern seen again and again in the Bible. God chose a tiny and insignificant people to come to know God over centuries of time. God chose an unknown young woman in a tiny country town. God chose a few small-town fishermen and a scorned tax collector. God's choices are radically unlike ours. Now the world will begin to understand.

I pointed out above that Paul found strength in his own weakness. So also he described the early church in similar terms:

Look at your situation when you were called, brothers and sisters! By ordinary human standards not many were wise, not many were powerful, not many were from the upper class. But God chose what the world considers foolish to shame the wise. God chose what the world considers weak to shame the strong. And God chose what the world considers low-class and low-life—what is considered to be nothing—to reduce what is considered to be something to nothing.

(1 Corinthians 1:26-28)

So whom does God consider important? It's obvious. The Bible drums the message in, and still we don't get it. We stick to our own standards and those of our community. We look at a big congregation with wealthy people and we call it important. We look at people at the head of big corporations—with compensation in the millions and mansions in wealthy suburbs and popular vacation areas—and call them "influential." We look at a wealthy country with powerful armies and think there is some relationship between that and God's values. But we can't do that if we really read the Bible and pay attention to its message: God puts down the mighty.

I'd say that's a warning to us all. It's a neat irony that we stamp "In God we trust" on every coin and bill in our pockets and wallets and purses, when it is in fact the money itself that we trust.

This country increasingly is governed by money. Increasingly only the wealthy and friends of the wealthy can run for high office. Increasingly our government policies are designed to protect the wealthy and enhance their wealth. Increasingly, our foreign policy is determined by our financial interests. The Middle East has oil, so we spend billions in an attempt to shape its destinies. Central Africa is impoverished, so whole populations can be dispossessed and decimated and we pay no attention. But that's about national policy, and I suspect political leaders pay less attention to human values than financial interests.

But what are God's values in this world? And what relationship is there between our values and God's? God, the Gospel today tells us, is probably more likely to care about a small congregation in a blighted part of the city or a struggling rural community than a large congregation with a paid choir and a reputation as "the place to go."

God is more likely, it seems to me, to care about the struggling victim of Alzheimer's disease confined to a wheelchair in a nursing home than the bishop or the Pope or the President. The Bible tells us about King Herod and the Roman Emperor only because they give us a date of reference for the time when God acted through two otherwise unknown women, changing the history of the world beyond what any king or emperor or politician or chief executive ever achieved.

And surely that is the drama we reenact every time we receive Communion. We receive a tiny piece of bread and a sip of wine, and in those symbols we are reminded of the reality of God's love. It's the same message again and again: You are important. You are important not for any talent or treasure you bring, but simply because you are God's own child, and you matter no more and no less than the two women whose story we read today.

The God who created this world was born in Bethlehem and died on a cross and conquered death simply for love of you.

Is each member of your congregation equally valued by the pastor, by the church committees, and by you?

GROUP STUDY GUIDE

Questions for Discussion

1. Who are the people in the world, in your community, or in your church who are usually considered "the least significant"?

2. Where and how do you normally expect to experience God at work in your life? How does this compare to the repeated biblical message that God works through the least?

3. If we see how God has worked in the past through the poor and small and insignificant, how can we see God at work today in the poor, or in refugees and immigrants seeking refuge in wealthy countries? How can we respond to God's work on the margins of power?

4. Are you more aware of God's presence in material things and physical events or in times of quiet and prayer? What is the difference?

5. How does the Christian message that God has become flesh in Jesus make the Christian faith different from other religions? What difference does it make in your own heart and life?

6. Is your community more influenced by financial interests or human values? Why? What about your church? Is it realistic to think that a local government or a nation's foreign policy can be influenced by biblical concerns?

7. Is there a tension in your congregation between "social activists" and those more centered on Bible study and prayer? Is it possible to balance these concerns in a constructive way?

8. What ordinary events in your own life have been occasions for God to work? Looking back, did you recognize that God was working at the time, or do you only recognize it in retrospect?

9. Realizing that God has worked in ordinary, everyday events, what hope do you have for the future?

Suggestions for Group Study

Where Is Bethlehem of Ephrathah?

Ask the group the following question: Where is our Bethlehem of Ephrathah? Brainstorm all of the places in your community that might be considered "unimportant" or "the least significant." Who or what is associated with those places? What makes them less important than other prominent locations or situations? Record and display your responses using a chalkboard, whiteboard, or projector screen, whatever is available. Discuss the following questions:

1. In what way is God working in these locations or circumstances? What good thing does God want us to take notice of there?

2. What are the centers of power in our community? What is the difference between these places and the ones we have just listed? What obstacles do they pose to God's work?

3. How can we become a part of the good work that God is doing in these least significant places? What will we have to change in our own hearts and lives in order to do so?

Pray for God to give you direction and attention as you seek to see God's love become incarnate among the least significant.

Pray With the Scriptures

There are many ways to read and interpret Scripture besides Bible study. *Lectio divina* is a traditional Christian way of reading the Scriptures, emphasizing quiet listening, contemplation, and responding prayerfully to God's Word. It is, in fact, a way of praying with a short Bible passage. Lectio divina, which literally means "divine reading," emphasizes hearing and receiving God's Word. The goal is not to search out meaning, whether historical, theological, or life application, as one would in a Bible study. Instead, the goal is simply to open your heart and mind to God, hearing what God has to say in this moment as you read the Scriptures. Lectio divina can be done individually or in small groups. In either case, the selected Bible passage is read slowly and out loud, followed by extended silence as the reader and others contemplate the Word they have just heard.

What follows are instructions for reading Mary's prayer in Luke 1:46-55 using lectio divina. You will read the passage slowly and out loud three times, followed by a period of silence each time.

Choose a reader who will read Luke 1:46-55. Have each group member close his or her eyes and take several deep breaths to enter a moment of silence. Instruct group members about what to listen for each time the passage is read. Then read through the passage aloud slowly three times, pausing for periods of silence between each reading.

The first time the passage is read, group members should listen for *a word, phrase, or image that stands out* as they hear the passage being read. What word does God lead them to focus on? After the reading, allow several long moments of silence for participants to think on the word or phrase they have been given. Then invite group members to speak the word or phrase out loud, if they wish. They should not offer any explanation or commentary, but simply speak the word or phrase.

For the second reading, group members should consider *how the word or phrase touches their heart or life that day.* How do they see Christ in the Scripture passage? Again, allow several long moments of silent reflection after the passage is read. After the silence, group members may share what they have noticed, but as before the sharing should be simple and brief.

For the third reading, group members should listen for *what God is calling them to do or be.* How do they see God inviting them to respond to the Scripture they have heard? After the period of silence, they may share what they have seen or heard.

Close the exercise by offering a short prayer, thanking God for speaking to the group through the Scriptures.

There are many ways to practice lectio divina in small groups or as individuals. For further information, see one of the following websites:

www.beliefnet.com/Faiths/Catholic/2000/08/How-To-Practice-Lectio-Divina.aspx

www.saintandrewsabbey.com/Lectio_Divina_s/267.htm

Closing Prayer

It is in small things and insignificant places and unimportant people, Lord God, that you have been at work to change history and transform our world. Open our eyes, we pray, to see your loving and creative hand at work, and close our eyes to the enticements of power. Draw us to share in the work you are doing. Give us strength to persevere when the way seems long and the obstacles too great to overcome, knowing that it is never our strength that matters and that the final victory will always be yours. Amen.

1 From *Tales of Hasidim: The Later Masters*, by Martin Buber (Schocken, 1948); pages 245–246.

2. From *The World is a Wedding*, by A. M. Allchin (Oxford University Press, 1978); page 45.

3. See *The Antichrist*, by F. W. Nietzsche, translated by H. L. Mencken (Knopf, 1920).

4. From *Readings in St. John's Gospel*, Volume 1, by William Temple (Macmillan and Co., 1939); page 20.

5. Dwight D. Eisenhower, from a speech before the American Society of Newspaper Editors, April 16, 1953, *www.informationclearinghouse.info/article9743.htm*. Accessed May 4, 2015.

6. From *Stride Toward Freedom: The Montgomery Story*, by Martin Luther King Jr. (Harper and Brothers, 1958); page 36.

Christmas Gifts

*Scriptures for
Christmas Day*
**Isaiah 9:2-7
Titus 2:11-14
Luke 2:1-20**

Some years ago, I lived in Japan and saw that Tokyo at Christmastime is not easily distinguished from Christmas time in any American city. Santa Claus was everywhere, and Christmas was commercialized as eagerly in Tokyo as in New York. Only about one to three percent of the Japanese population is formally connected to any Christian church, but it is customary in Japan to give employees a very large bonus at the end of the year, and merchants are very interested in finding ways to transfer that money from the employees' pockets to their cash registers. What works in New York works just as well in Tokyo: Santa Claus is the answer!

One year, one of the larger department stores in Tokyo put posters in the display areas above the windows in buses and subways with a side view of a young woman lying naked and face down on a sandy beach. Above her was the word *Christmas* and below her was the word *love*. Christmas and love are, of course, closely related subjects, but the research department had not, apparently, fully analyzed the nature of that relationship. Japan's small Christian community thought the picture did not fairly reflect the theme of the season as they understood it, and they registered vigorous protests that got the department store's attention. The ads were withdrawn. The merchandising of Christmas continued, of course, in other ways.

But how well do we who are Christians understand God's love for us as expressed in the birth of Jesus? We have been searching the Scriptures for four weeks now as we seek to prepare ourselves to celebrate Christmas with deeper understanding. We have looked at the words of the prophets spoken centuries before Jesus' birth; we have looked at the stories told about the events that took place immediately before that birth; and we have studied the attempts made by Paul and the early Christian church to explain its meaning. In all this, we have noticed the way "hope" gets our attention again and again.

Now, we come to celebrate Christmas Day itself, and we are given one more set of readings to study. But can any three short paragraphs fully explain why Christmas has become a worldwide phenomenon and Christianity a faith that has transformed millions upon millions of lives? The phenomenon of Christmas in Japan makes it clear that the message is often garbled and misunderstood. That is nothing new. The first settlers in New England felt that the English celebration of Christmas in their day had become so distorted that they outlawed the celebration of Christmas in New England entirely. The joy of Christmas, nevertheless, seems to break through all our restrictions and misinterpretations; it insists on some kind of celebration, however far from the point. So we as Christians, all of us, have a job to do: We must hear and express the words we are given in these readings so that we can help others hear them with deeper understanding and share with us the hope we find in the birth of Jesus today, not only as we celebrate it in our churches, but also as we live it out in our daily lives.

Now that we are coming to the end of our journey, it's a good time to go back to the question posed at the outset: What symbol or image best expresses the hope reflected in our Advent Scriptures? Is hope, indeed, an anchor for your life, or is it a "thing with feathers" that "perches in the soul"? Or is hope something different altogether? Do you have a way of thinking about hope that is both helpful to you and consistent with the way it is portrayed in the Bible?

ISAIAH 9:2-7

Faith, hope, and love, said the apostle Paul, are the great virtues, "and the greatest of these is love" (1 Corinthians 13:13). Yes, but each has a critical role to play, and hope alone looks forward. The first reading for Christmas Day takes us back more than seven centuries and shows us the power of hope as it takes the simplest of human events, the birth of a child, and invests it with the power to call us forward to the transformation of all human life forever.

"A child is born to us, a son is given to us" (Isaiah 9:6). The text is reporting an event that has already taken place, not something centuries in the future, yet Christians have always recognized that it was speaking of the birth of Jesus. How do we get from there to here?

Scholars tell us that these words come to us from a time in the history of Israel when hope was in short supply. The northern regions, those around the Sea of Galilee, had been conquered by Assyrian forces moving down from the north and threatening Jerusalem itself. But a royal child had been born, and that birth is celebrated in these verses as a sign of good things to come. New life has come into the world, bringing new hope with it. More than seven centuries before the birth of Jesus, a child was born who brought renewed hope into the world. Of course, we might say that this happens all the time and there is nothing remarkable about it. That is true, but this time the hope that was born was celebrated in words that resonated far beyond the particular event.

Notice, first of all, that this passage is not, as so much of the Bible is, God's Word to us but rather our words to God. There is no "thus says the Lord" to mark this as a prophetic utterance of God's judgment or promise. Rather, the words are addressed to God and celebrate what God has done for the people: "You [God] have made the nation great; you have increased its joy" (Isaiah 9:3).

What has God done to earn this tribute? Sent a newborn child! But because of that birth there is hope for people who have been "walking in darkness" and "living in a pitch-dark land" (verse 2). Scholars disagree as to who the royal child may have been and offer at least three different possibilities for interpreting the event celebrated here. It may have been the birth of Hezekiah, who reigned from 715 to 687 B.C., or it may have been the birth of a son of Hezekiah. It is also possible that the song was celebrating not the birth, but the coronation of Hezekiah. One way or another, however, it is a song of hope, hope vested in a frail human being, whether a newborn infant or a newly crowned king. So long as infants are born and new leaders come into office, there is hope: Life can change, the darkness can come to an end, and light can dawn once again. In America, such hopes rise and fall in a four-year cycle with every presidential election.

Like the people of ancient Israel, we tend to set our hopes in human leaders too high, and we are disappointed again and again.

We might ask whether the language here is so "over the top" that disappointment is inevitable but, in fact, the sheer exuberance of the language makes it plain that no human being can possibly fulfill such hopes. The result is that we must look to God to act through human agents and, indeed, to come to us in a human being. Who but God in human flesh, God incarnate, can fulfill the hopes and expectations raised by these words?

Thus it came about that this short passage was cherished all the more as hopes were disappointed, and expectations were raised for a future Messiah who could fulfill the hopes here expressed. No wonder hope rose ever higher as the years and centuries passed; no wonder Christians looked at this passage and saw a vision that only the incarnate Son of God could fulfill.

But has the vision been fulfilled? It is hard to read this passage without hearing the music of Handel's *Messiah*, and that triumphant music itself raises our hopes further still. Such glorious language and such inspiring music require a wonderful object indeed. Yet we, like the people of Palestine in the first century, are entitled to feel that we are not there yet, that the vision has raised our sights beyond what has been accomplished. Where is the reign of peace that will have no end? Where is the righteousness and justice we long for and have been promised?

There is no easy answer to these questions. We could simply say that our hopes are still disappointed, and there would be much truth in that. We could say that these verses themselves are, in part, responsible for that disappointment because they raise our hopes to an unrealistic height. But is the fault with the verses or with us? Should we not set our hopes at this height? Should we settle for something less? Do these verses not express God's purpose for us? And has not God in Christ both shown us what we are to be and provided for us grace and guidance toward that goal?

What is clear is that these verses continue to resonate and to inspire us. The centuries pass and our failures mount, but as often as we read this passage and as often as we celebrate the birth of Jesus, the hope is renewed. Faith and love endure but hope continues to call us forward—and not simply because an inspired poet wrote these words long ago, but because God has acted in the birth of Jesus to show us the vision in human flesh and to challenge us to let Christ be born also in us. Only when we do so will the world be able to see in us the reality of God's incarnate love and rejoice with us in that gift.

What answer do we have for those without hope? Are we ourselves too likely to give up hope for ourselves, our church, our world? How can we use faith and love to keep hope alive?

TITUS 2:11-14

Set between the two great outbursts of joy in Isaiah and Luke, the brief passage from the Epistle to Titus exhorting us to live "sensible, ethical, and godly lives" seems an odd choice for the great celebration of Christmas. How often, one wonders, will you hear a Christmas sermon on this text? How often will those who hear it take time to ponder it or go home meditating on it?

But consider the power packed in these few words. Allied forces dropped some four thousand tons of bombs on Dresden in mid-February, 1945, but one single bomb weighing less than five tons did far more damage to Hiroshima a few months later. Great power can be packed into a relatively small container. So in these few short verses there is enormous power. The bombs dropped on Dresden and Hiroshima brought death, but the power concentrated in these few short verses brings life.

Over the last four weeks, we have seen how hope has been given to God's people in various times and places. We have hope because God has acted in the past, because God acts in us now, and because God will act decisively in time to come. All this is contained in this short reading from the Epistle to Titus, and hope is at the center of the stage. We are told that the "grace of God" has appeared, changing our lives now even as we wait in hope for Christ to come again:

The grace of God *has appeared*, bringing salvation to all people . . . so that we can live sensible, ethical, and godly lives *right now*. . . . At the same time *we wait* for the blessed hope and the glorious appearance of our great God and savior Jesus Christ.

(Titus 2:11-13, emphasis added)

We might have expected that the reading for Christmas Day would make direct reference to the story of Christ's birth, but the Epistles are not concerned to tell again the story of Jesus' birth nor, indeed, to tell any stories of his life. It seems likely, in fact, that most of the Epistles were written before there were any finished Gospels. Paul and others had, of course, told the story of Christ's death and resurrection, but their immediate focus was on the power and meaning of those events and their impact on the lives of those who heard their message. Nowhere is that summed up more succinctly and powerfully than here.

Many New Testament experts tell us that this letter was likely not written by Paul himself, but by someone else writing in Paul's name. They tell us that it may have been written as many as fifty years after Paul's death. One might think that if half a century had gone by, the intense focus on waiting for Christ's second coming would have faded, but there is no evidence of that here. The hope of that event remains central to this passage as, indeed, hope must remain central to Christians living today.

Notice also how the author speaks of Jesus in these early days of the church. Some have argued that it took many generations for Christians to speak definitely of Jesus' divinity, but here he is called "our great God and savior Jesus Christ" (verse 13).

So God has appeared and will come again, but meanwhile we have lives to live, and those lives must be transformed by Christ in us now. As the great fourteenth-century mystic, Meister Eckhart, pointed out, Christ's birth in Bethlehem makes little difference unless he is also born in each of us.[1] The vivid portrayal of a child in a manger found on the typical Christmas card can distance Jesus from us. The romantic picture of the manger surrounded by humble shepherds and bewildered animals is too different from anything familiar to us. We can look at it as if through a temporal telescope, seeing the manger scene as a distant event and never thinking of the consequences for our lives today. But that birth, that coming of a Savior, must be constantly renewed, and there must be consequences. Those consequences are spelled out in a few clear, strong words.

The Epistle tells us that "the grace of God . . . educates us," and it does so in three ways (verses 11-12). The three terms laid out here are

THE GIFT OF NEW HOPE

carefully chosen to include every aspect of our lives. The Common English Bible says our lives must be "sensible, ethical, and godly." Other widely used translations, the New Revised Standard Version and New International Version, say, "self-controlled, upright, and godly," and that may make it clearer that we have responsibilities to ourselves, to others, and to God.

First, we have a responsibility to ourselves; Christ came for each of us and wants us to come to him. We can come, indeed, "just as I am," in the words of the familiar hymn,[2] but then we must be changed, renewed, washed, transformed by the grace of God at work in our lives. Lives transformed by Christ are characterized by self-control, daily choosing to follow Christ rather than the "desires of this world" (verse 12). Christ in you has to make a difference.

Second, we must act toward others in a way that makes a difference in the world. The words *ethical* and *upright* imply setting an example, but it is more than that. The passage ends with the expectation that we will be "eager to do good actions" (verse 14). Other translations speak of "good deeds" (NRSV) and even "good works" (KJV), which may worry those who remember how Christians have fought over the relationship between faith and works in past centuries. But there is no implication here that we can earn salvation by "good actions." The point is that those who have been given the gift of life through faith should be eager to serve others as Christ served us. We are, indeed, saved by faith, but faith has consequences; our faith should become evident in our actions. So these few verses not only sum up what God has done, is doing, and will do among us, but also how we are to respond. If we are chosen to be God's special people, we must respond by living lives transformed in every way.

Third, we are to be "godly." Many understand this to mean something like "devout," "religious," or "holy," but the simple meaning of the word is "god-like," and that has much larger implications than mere piety. The overwhelming truth is that we are called to belong to God and to be like God, and that means far more than "being religious." To be "God-like" is to care for the whole world as God cares for the whole of creation. It is an impossible demand—except that God comes to us to enable us to carry it out, to make the impossible possible. If we are called to be God-like, there is no limit to the demand but also no limit to the help available.

Hope remains at the center of the stage. The challenge is almost beyond imagining, but so is the reality of God's presence in our lives. Christmas is not an end but a beginning, looking forward always to a fulfillment. Especially on Christmas Day hope is central. As children's hopes are fulfilled under the Christmas tree, they learn the joy of hope satisfied. As adults, we learn to grow in grace and look forward joyfully to the fulfillment of hope in union with the God who made us for that destiny.

How can you hold on to the central hope and power of Christ's coming in the midst of our narrow and immediate hopes for gifts, food, and reunions?

LUKE 2:1-20

I grew up in a very small town and my father was in charge of three small-town churches. Each of these, of course, needed a service on Christmas Day, so our home celebration was delayed until he returned from the last service of Christmas morning. Meanwhile, we were given a few small gifts in our stockings; but the Christmas tree, with most of the gifts, was closed off by the doors to the living room. But even when the doors to that room were finally opened, there was no rush to tear open the gifts. Instead, we followed a prescribed order: The first gift under the tree was chosen by the youngest child to give to someone else. Not until it was opened and admired could the next youngest child choose a gift for someone else. Thus, one by one, the gifts were distributed and opened until there were none left. Friends would come by to ask whether we could come out and play, but they were told, "No, we are still opening presents." Our friends had long since opened and probably broken their gifts, but we were still at it! They probably thought we were overwhelmed with gifts, since it took us so long to unwrap them. Our fulfillment was long delayed, but there was great satisfaction in imagining the enormous pile of gifts that our friends must have envisioned.

The Gospel reading for Christmas Day might be seen as a great pile of gifts to be opened and appreciated one by one. Unlike the concentrated power of the Epistle reading, the Gospel gives us a long and wandering narrative with attention concentrated first on Caesar,

THE GIFT OF NEW HOPE

then on Mary and Joseph in their journey, then on the birth of the Child, then on the manger, then on the shepherds on the hillside, then on the angels, then on the shepherds' journey, and at last we are left with the shepherds proclaiming and Mary pondering the meaning of this strange but ordinary series of events. The impact of all these events cannot be absorbed in one day or one year or even a lifetime.

First, then, we might consider the sheer range of the story, which extends not simply from Caesar in his palace to the homeless family in the manger behind the inn, but from the angels of heaven itself to the humble, newborn child. Could even the most imaginative Hollywood screenwriter craft such a drama?

We have time here to open only a few of the gifts we are given. Consider for one the point John Calvin noticed: All doors were closed to the Holy Family, but by Jesus' birth heaven itself is opened to us.[3] That is a gift.

Unwrap the angel's words, "I bring good news to you—wonderful, joyous news for all people" (Luke 2:10). The news is very personal, it comes "to you," but it is unlimited in its reach, which is "for all people." That also is a gift.

Unwrap the titles the angel announces: "savior . . . Christ . . . Lord" (verse 11). Lancelot Andrewes, chair of the committee that made the King James Version of the Bible, said that when we are in trouble, "There is no joy in the earth to the joy of a Saviour."[4] Christ is a title so familiar we forget it is the Greek word for the Hebrew word *Messiah* and the English phrase *Anointed One*. Each of these has a somewhat different flavor, but collectively they speak of one with authority, and in our chaotic times we look in vain for human authority to deal with the dangers surrounding us. "Lord" has become a controversial term, but the new Presbyterian hymnal, *Glory to God*, points out that "when the writers of the New Testament confess Jesus to be Lord, they thereby proclaim that not Caesar, but Christ rules this world."[5] The angels are making a statement: It's a gift to know Christ is Savior and Lord.

Then there's the angels' proclamation of glory to God and peace on earth (verse 14). T.S. Eliot, in his play *Murder in the Cathedral*, has Archbishop Thomas á Becket preach on this text and say:

Reflect now, how Our Lord Himself spoke of Peace. He said to His disciples, 'My peace I leave with you, my peace I give unto you.' Did He mean peace as we think of it: the kingdom of England at peace with its neighbours, the barons at peace with the King, the householder counting over his peaceful gains, the swept hearth, his best wine for a friend at the table, his wife singing to the children? Those men His disciples knew no such things: they went forth to journey afar, to suffer by land and sea, to know torture, imprisonment, disappointment, to suffer death by martyrdom. What then did He mean? If you ask that, remember then that He said also, 'Not as the world gives, give I unto you.' So then, He gave to His disciples peace, but not peace as the world gives.[6]

A hymn written by William Alexander Percy a hundred years ago tells how Peter was crucified and John died in exile. It describes God's peace as "strife closed in the sod," but implores us nonetheless to pray for "the marvelous peace of God."[7]

Peace is a great gift, but we are often surprised by what we find when we unwrap it. Our hopes may not correspond to "the peace of God that exceeds all understanding," but we are promised nevertheless that it "will keep your hearts and minds safe in Christ Jesus" (Philippians 4:7). Often, the hope for peace presents us with a choice to make between peace as we think of it and peace which is "not peace as the world gives."

Finally, for all the simplicity of the manger scene and familiarity of a child's birth, what God has done and is doing remains a mystery beyond our understanding. Unwrap as much as we can, there is always more. We should pay attention to a point made by Mark Frank, a seventeenth-century English scholar, who tells us that in all our unwrapping of gifts and revealing of contents, Christmas remains "a day of mysteries." As he says, "It is a mysterious business we are about; Christ wrapped up, Christ in the sacrament, Christ in a mystery; let us be content to let it go so, believe, admire, and adore. . . . "[8]

Worship is the only truly adequate response. But that worship is centered on One who came, as we must also do, to love and serve a world divided from its Creator and in need of God's love and ours. Hope at last is neither an insubstantial wish nor a philosophy, but a person. Christ, in the beginning and at the end, is our hope.

What hope do you find in the Nativity story?

GROUP STUDY GUIDE

Questions for Discussion

1. The readings for Christmas are three very different passages: a hymn of praise (Isaiah), a concise theological statement (Titus), and a story (Luke). Which of the three readings is most memorable? Why?

2. Reread Isaiah 9:2-7 and list the various hopeful events you see there. Consider the historical circumstances in which this message was delivered. What might Isaiah's audience have thought upon hearing these words? What is your response to them?

3. Do you agree that the high hopes in Isaiah 9:2-7 are, in a sense, beyond us? To what extent have they been fulfilled in Christ? In what ways are we still waiting for their fulfillment?

4. Think about hope in terms of the figures mentioned in Luke 2:1-20. What did Mary hope for, what did the shepherds hope for, and what did the angels hope for? What other people are mentioned, and what might their hopes have been?

5. How did the hopes of these individuals change through the event of Jesus' birth?

6. Besides those discussed above, what other "gifts" do you find in Luke's Nativity story? Which of them has the most power to change your heart and life right now?

7. At Advent and Christmas we uncover a tension between the past and the future: Christ has come to fulfill God's promises to us, and Christ will come again to bring those promises to completion. Based on the Titus reading, how are we called to live "in the meantime"? What does this look like in practice in the present day?

8. Where and how do we find peace? Is it internal and personal, or is it a hope for our community or for the world? What can your local church do to make peace a reality today?

9. The opening paragraphs of this book posed the question whether an anchor or feathered bird or something else was the better symbol of hope. How have the Advent Bible passages altered your perception of hope? What symbol of hope best reflects what we find in the Scriptures?

10. What new hope have you discovered for yourself, your church, or the world over the last several weeks? How will you carry this hope forward through the upcoming year?

Suggestions for Group Study

How Far Is It to Bethlehem?

A modern Christmas carol asks, "How far is it to Bethlehem?" and answers, "Not very far." But is that always the case? Mary and Joseph journeyed down from Nazareth, about eighty-five miles. The shepherds came from the surrounding fields, a much shorter journey. Matthew, however, tells of magi who came "from the East," implying a much greater distance. But distances are psychological as well as physical. Some of us have found it a short journey to come to worship Jesus as Lord, but for others of us it may take many long years and include many wrong turns.

Give each group member a piece of paper, and ask participants to sketch their faith journey. The "destination" will be the manger, where we worship the newborn king. Note that not everyone will feel that they have arrived; make it clear that this is OK. Instruct group members to consider their starting point, wanderings along the way, barriers or obstacles to overcome, guideposts, fellow travelers, and so forth. Participants may find it useful to identify with the shepherds, the magi, Mary and Joseph, or some other figure in the Christmas story.

Invite anyone who wishes to share his or her sketch to do so, recognizing that some may prefer not to share. Discuss how group members, and the congregation as a whole, can be of help to others on their journey. How can participants remove obstacles for one another, or help one another get past them? How can you provide announcements such as the one the angel gave the shepherds, or point to guiding stars such as the one the magi followed?

Choose Hope

The nineteenth-century philosopher/theologian Søren Kierkegaard described the contrast between hope and despair. Hope, he says, expects the good, while despair or fear expects evil. To hope is a decision we must make, sometimes daily.

Divide into three teams and assign one of today's Scripture passages to each group: Team One will consult Isaiah 9:2-7; Team Two will consult Titus 2:11-14; and Team Three will consult Luke 2:1-20. Have each team read and discuss their assigned reading, making note of any words or phrases that will help them make the decision to choose hope. Allow five to ten minutes for teams to work, then gather back together for each team to share their findings. What words or phrases stood out to each team, and why were those particularly useful to help us choose hope?

Consider having one or more group members write a short reflection based on these insights, which can be shared with the rest of the congregation in the church newsletter.

Closing Prayer

You have filled us, eternal and loving God, with hope for ourselves and our world and your church. We have learned to see you at work in history, and we know that you are drawing all things toward your purpose. Help us, we pray, to be people prepared to put aside all concern for ourselves and to offer ourselves ever more completely for your purpose. Open our eyes to your work in the world; open our hearts to your presence in our lives; open our hands to make them available to serve you where the need is greatest. Let our hope be centered on you alone, and let us meet you and serve you throughout your world.

1. From *The Mystical Thought of Meister Eckhart: The Man From Whom God Hid Nothing*, by Bernard McGinn (Herder & Herder, 2001); pages 116–117.
2. From "Just as I Am, Without One Plea," words by Charlotte Elliott, *The United Methodist Hymnal* (The United Methodist Publishing House, 1989); 357.
3. From *A Harmony of the Gospels, Matthew, Mark and Luke*, by John Calvin, translated by A. W. Morrison (St. Andrew Press, 1972); page 73.
4. From *Sermons on the Nativity*, by Lancelot Andrewes (Baker Book House, 1955); page 74.
5. From *Glory to God* (Westminster John Knox Press, 2013); page 930.
6. From *Murder in the Cathedral*, by T. S. Eliot (Harcourt Brace & Co., 1935); page 48.
7. From "They Cast Their Nets in Galilee," *The Hymnal 1982* (The Church Hymnal Corporation); 661.
8. From *LI Sermons*, by Mark Frank (Andrew Clark, 1672); page 90.